# What Others Are Saying About Rent-to-*Sell*...

*"With Rent-to-Sell, Wendy Patton offers a timeless, proven solution to getting your house sold so you can move on to your next opportunity. It's a strategic must-read for sellers seeking creative options and the real estate agents that support them.*
**Gary Keller**
**New York Times best-selling author of SHIFT:**
**How Top Real Estate Agents Tackle Tough Times**

*"Wendy Patton hit the nail on the head with this one. Wendy covers every aspect from preparing your house for sale to the nitty-gritty paperwork. Wendy is truly a remarkable lady who is more qualified than anyone to teach on this subject. In fact, I would tell you that YOU'RE CRAZY if you don't read this book because it is the most detailed book I have ever seen on the subject...period!*
**Than Merrill**
**Real Estate Investor, Founder of FortuneBuilders.com and**
**Star of A&E's "Flip this House"**

*"Ta daaa... a real "how to" book that covers the creative methods of selling with tremendous detail from "A to Z". It is a survival manual for the Real Estate Professional and the seller."*
**Kathleen Sanchez**
**Associate Broker/Owner**
**Coldwell Banker Shooltz**

*"Wow, talk about timing! This book must be read now by anyone trying to sell their home or any real estate agent that wants to serve their clients more effectively."*
**David Lindahl**
**Real Estate Investment Expert (ReMentor.com)**
**Best Selling Author of Emerging Real Estate Markets and Multi Family**
**Millions and www.rementor.com**

D0189961

# Rent To Sell

## Your Hands-on Guide to *Sell* Your Home When Buyers Are Scarce

**Wendy Patton**

*AuthorHouse™*
*1663 Liberty Drive, Suite 200*
*Bloomington, IN 47403*
*www.authorhouse.com*
*Phone: 1-800-839-8640*

*First published by AuthorHouse 2/2/09*

*ISBN: 978-1-4389-5320-5 (sc)*
*Library of Congress Control Number: 2009900918*

*Printed in the United States of America*
*Bloomington, Indiana*

*This book is printed on acid-free paper.*

# Rent-To-Sell

**Your Hands-on Guide to *Sell* Your Home
When Buyers Are Scarce**

# TABLE OF CONTENTS

What Others Are Saying About *Rent-to-Sell*....................…..iii
Introduction........................................................…..…..ix
Dedication ….…..................,.…................................…..vii

**PART 1: WHAT IS RENT-TO-OWN AND HOW DOES IT WORK?**

**Chapter 1: What is Rent-To-Own?**........................................1

*An explanation of what rent-to-own is and how it can apply to home sellers and the real estate agents who represent them. How renting-to-own can be so useful in today's depressed real estate markets.*

Why would I need to do this rent-to-own thing?....................2
When will rent-to-own NOT work?......................................12

**Chapter 2: How Does Renting-To-Own Work?**...................15

*An overview of the rent-to-own process while explaining key fundamentals*

Understanding Rent-to-Own.......................................…..15
How rent-to-own transactions are structured The Contracts
How rent-to-own transactions are structured – the Terms

**PART 2: PREPARING AND MARKETING YOUR HOME**

**Chapter 3: Repairs - Three Strikes and You're Out!**..........29

*Choosing what repairs should be done on a limited budget. Also, what if you can't afford to do any repairs.*

**Chapter 4: Curb Appeal and Home Staging –
Getting the Most Bling for the Buck** ...........................53

*Using simple staging techniques or using the services of professional home stagers to maximize your price and place a tenant-buyer quickly*

**Chapter 5: Pricing and Rental Rates**...........................81

*Over or under pricing your home can either cause it to languish on the market or cost you thousands, if not tens of thousands, of dollars. The same goes for accurately setting rental rates. How a little research can make a big difference.*

**Chapter 6: Using a Realtor®**.....................................91

*Yes, you have to pay them a commission. A good real estate agent will earn their commission many times over in the services and time savings they provide you. How do you find and screen a good Realtor®?*

**Chapter 7: Marketing - Signs & Flyers,**
**Newspaper & Internet, Word of Mouth**......................101

*Street level marketing lets nearby people know about your home and can be an excellent way to generate calls and showings. The newspaper is the old-reliable way of advertising but can get expensive. The internet can provide great exposure often at far less cost. Word of Mouth is free and sometimes can work wonders. Where to get exposure for FREE. Also, how to advertise and market for buyers instead of marketing your home.*

## PART 3: UNDERSTANDING THE PAPERWORK

**Chapter 8: Rental Agreements**..................................113

*Many people think all rental agreements are the same, but they don't have to be. Key aspects to include and pitfalls to avoid.*

**Chapter 9: Option Agreements** ..........................121
*An overview of important aspects to include in the option agreement.*

**Chapter 10: Sales Contract**....................................129
*Like lease agreements, not all sales contracts are the same. Key aspects to include and avoid in sales contracts.*

**Chapter 11: Memorandum of Option**........................137
*Is this something we use when we are the seller and what does it mean to us and to our buyer?*

**PART 4: RECEIVING AN OFFER AND NEGOTIATIONS**

**Chapter 12: Key Points to Negotiate –
Not All Dealsare Created Equal**...................................143

*Focusing on key aspects that can make huge differences in
the terms of the deal for the seller.*

**Chapter 13: Negotiating Tips**........................................155

*Tips for increasing the strength of your negotiations and
ways to counter some standard negotiation points.*

**Chapter 14: Qualifying Tenant-Buyers**........................169

*Tips for properly screening and financially qualifying your
tenant-buyer.*

**Chapter 15: Fair Housing Law**.....................................185

*An explanation of how Fair Housing Law applies to you, and
how to stay compliant and out of any trouble*

Set Your Standards in Writing.....................................187
Common Mistakes......................................................188

**Chapter 16: Approved! – What do I do Next?**...................193

*A step-by-step checklist for placing your tenant-buyer in your
rent-to-own home*

# PART 5: WHAT TO DO DURING THE RENT-TO-OWN AND HOW TO CLOSE THE DEAL

**Chapter 17: Making Sure Everyone Gets Paid** ............209

*Important components to making sure the tenant is paying rent and how you can protect yourself. Who pays for what during the rent-to-own period?*

**Chapter 18: How to Help Your Buyers Qualify for a Mortgage**...........................................215

*Information about how buyers can improve their credit so they can qualify for financing when it comes time to buy the home; including working with a mortgage broker to become a home owner. Creating a paper trail with checks to help secure financing.*

**Chapter 19: Oops, Not Everything Went to Plan**..........225

*How to handle lease extensions and pricing and terms modifications to the original deal. What if you need to do an eviction?*

**Chapter 20: Completing the Transaction and Selling Your Home**.................................................239

*An overview of completing the sale. The closing table and what is involved when picking up your check.*

## PART 6: PRACTICAL ADVICE

**Chapter 21: Important Components to Get Right
So You Can Maintain Your Sanity**..........................251

*Important details to make sure things go smoothly and ways to add peace of mind and reduce stress during the process.*

## PART 7: FOR THE REAL ESTATE AGENT ONLY

**Chapter 22: When and How to Recommend
Renting-to-Own to Your Seller** ...........................261

*An overview of how to explain a new way of thinking to your sellers.*

**Chapter 23: Having the Rewards and Risks
Discussion with Your Seller** .......................................269

*Important CYA (Cover Your Assets) clauses to have your seller sign. Why these are important to you and your brokerage.*

**Chapter 24: How to Get Paid Your Entire Commission
And More** ......................................................277

*Strategies for getting your entire commission, and possibly more, when you help your sellers complete a rent-to-own transaction.*

# Dedication

This book is dedicated to all of the sellers in North America that need to sell their home. Unfortunately, the real estate markets have changed in most parts of the country and we too must change our thinking, our strategies and our approaches to the way we do things.

This includes selling our homes. I congratulate you for picking up this book and thinking differently from your competition. This book is also dedicated to the real estate professionals that must change the way they do business in order to survive this real estate downturn. Congratulations to you for picking up this book and making a change in your business approach.

I want to give special thanks to so many people that helped me with this book. Robert Golden, I couldn't do it without you! To my friends and colleagues Debbie Kessler, Beth Slade, Merrilee Anderson, and Julie Greenhill, that helped me with reading and proofing my writings over and over again, thanks. To my husband, Michael, who has to put up without me during the times when I am writing. I appreciate you all so much.

# Introduction

Let me paint a picture for you. You have been trying to sell your home for a while. You spent a lot of time and effort cleaning it up and making it presentable. You may have even spent a lot of money fixing it up to make things look brand new. Of course, you aren't the only one trying to sell. There are probably more for sale signs in your neighborhood than you can ever remember.

If you listed your home with a real estate agent they probably gave you a lot of suggestions on how to make your home even more presentable. After more time, effort and most likely money, you probably had some showings initially but no offers, or at least no reasonable offers. The effort you put into cleaning up your house and having it "just so" for each showing has just become more pain and disappointment when the showing turns into another "no offer" effort. After a while, the number of showings have slowed to a trickle or stopped altogether. Your real estate agent starts talking about a price reduction. Maybe it is taking longer to get a return phone call, and when they do call back, you get the same story on how the market has slowed down, and they ask for your patience. Your home's listing agreement is getting close to expiring and you are trying to decide what to do. Maybe your real estate agent gave you this book to consider an alternative. If they did, thank them for being creative and helping you in a difficult time to consider your options. Do yourself and your agent a favor, read the book.

If you went the "For Sale by Owner" route, you got even fewer showings but received TONS of phone calls from real estate agents trying to get the listing. There may have been some calls from investors hoping to wrangle the deal of the century out of you.

Either way you are frustrated because you want to SELL your home. You didn't put it on the market for the fun of it. You have plans and you want to move on.

Odds are that if you are reading this you have already experienced one of the two above scenarios. Let me reassure you, you aren't alone. Much of the country is going through a real estate crunch right now and home sellers across the country are experiencing the pains of trying to sell their home.

As of September of 2008, the National Association of Realtors® (NAR) reported that the current month's supply of homes across the nation is 9.9 months. That means at the current pace of sales, it will take 9.9 months to sell all of the homes on the market. A balanced real estate market typically has about 6 months supply, which means we've got an extra 4 months of surplus homes to get sold. That's a lot of competition for the small pool of buyers out there.

Naturally, more homes are coming on the market, and it looks like it's only going to get worse for a while as the foreclosure volume from the subprime mess is still increasing. In fact, RealtyTrac®[i] reported that in the 1st quarter of 2008 foreclosure filings were up 116% over the 1st quarter of 2007. And by October of 2008, RealtyTrac® reported that foreclosures were up 25% for the month over 2007 and were 5% higher than September of 2008. By the end of the year they predict that nearly 1/3 of all properties on the market will be foreclosures.

Homeowners and banks aren't the only ones trying to sell their houses. New home builders overbuilt in many areas. They have brand new homes completed and just sitting there. These builders are desperate to find buyers. Throw them into the mix and the picture doesn't look too pretty does it?

If it were a reality TV show they would call it "Lost! The Search for America's Home Buyers."

The advantage you have over all of these other home-burdened souls is that you are now reading this! Does reading this guarantee that your home is going to get sold? No. But it does give you a HUGE advantage over the countless numbers of other home sellers out there right now and let's face it, with this many homes on the market, you need every advantage you can get.

If you happen to be reading this before you've actually tried to put your home on the market – congratulations! – you are way ahead of the game.

This *is* a guide to getting your home sold in a market where homes just aren't selling or a way to sell your home quicker and possibly for more money in areas where homes are still selling. This is a guide to a creative home selling technique known as rent-to-own or lease with an option to buy.

Selling your home on a rent-to-own basis is nothing new. People have been doing it for decades. In fact, the very first recorded example of a rent-to-own transaction in the United States is when George Washington rented and then purchased Mount Vernon from Thomas Jefferson.

Just kidding. It was Benjamin Franklin. That's why his picture is on the $100 bill and Washington is only on the $1 bill, because ole Ben knew how to make the big bucks.

Okay, so I made that up. But the point is that rent-to-own is certainly nothing new. We aren't inventing the wheel here. It's just that it's become a little bit less commonplace in the last decade or so. The reason for that is very simple – for the last decade the banks made it their personal goal to give a mortgage to every man, woman and child on the face of the earth that could pass one simple test – could they fog a mirror when they breathed on it. As long as the applicant was alive the banks didn't see any reason to bother with things like income, down payments, appraisals based on reality, etc.

Poor George, he looks awfully lonely.

Naturally this couldn't last forever. From the massive volume of "for sale" signs plastered on everyone's front lawn we can see that it hasn't. Now the banks are only willing to give mortgages to applicants if they can provide a 90% upfront down payment and are willing to give their first born up to indentured servitude until the loan is paid off.

Yes, I'm exaggerating. If you've been trying to sell your home in this buyer-scarce market, that's exactly what it feels like. The point I'm making is that it is much, MUCH harder to get a loan than it used to be.

As I said, renting-to-own had become a little less commonplace, but it's time to dust it off and put it back into mainstream practice. In the upcoming chapters I will teach you what rent-to-own is, how it works and lots of other tips and tricks for getting YOUR home sold when your neighbors can't. Yes, you can tell them about this great technique to help them sell their house too, but I would wait until you've gotten a rent-to-own buyer for your house first.

Before we jump into all of the details, you are probably wondering, "How hard is this going to be?" Maybe you are wondering if this is something you can do on your own or if buying this book is going to be a big waste of money. Since you've been patient enough to read through this whole introduction I'm going to reward you with that answer. If you happen to have skipped ahead right to the end of the introduction, you sneaky devil you, you're in luck, you'll get the answer too…

I can safely say that you are definitely not wasting your money. I've got two kids in college right now, and given the cost of college tuition (times 2!) you can rest assured that your money is going to a good cause.

Seriously, though, I have been doing rent-to-own deals for more than 20 years. That's right, I was doing them before the bankers stole all of the good buyers. And yes, I still did them while the banks were trying to fulfill their goal of eliminating all renters on the planet by digging themselves into the subprime pit of doom. Fortunately for me I outlived a lot of these banks. Not only have I been doing rent-to-own transactions through all of this, but I've also been teaching others to do them as well. I have taught more than 20,000 people from all walks of life and I can assure you that I wouldn't still be teaching if it couldn't be learned.

So, if you've already bought this book, go ahead and get comfortable in your favorite chair, put your feet up and we'll get started. If you haven't bought this yet, but you have a home to sell, trust me, this will come in VERY handy. In fact, given the current market, it just may be the only way you'll get your home sold right now. Go ahead and proceed to the cashier and fork over your credit card, my kids' university thanks you!

*Wendy*

---

[i] RealtyTrac is the only major real estate website to feature foreclosure, auction, bank-owned, for-sale-by-owner, resale MLS and new construction properties. RealtyTrac is also the leading online marketplace for foreclosure properties and publishes the country's largest, most comprehensive foreclosure database, with more than 1.5 million default, auction and bank-owned homes from across the country.

# PART 1:

## WHAT IS RENT-TO-OWN AND HOW DOES IT WORK?

# Chapter 1

# What is Rent-to-Own?

Before we can look at the reason for wanting to sell as well as how to sell your home on a rent-to-own basis, we first need to understand what rent-to-own is. A rent-to-own can also be referred to as a Lease with an Option to Buy, a Lease Option, a Lease to Own, etc. In this book we will call it a rent-to-own, but these words can be used interchangeably and you will want to use whatever phrase is most used or understood in your part of the country. In a nutshell, a rent-to-own sale means you are allowing your future buyer to live in the home for a period as a tenant (or renter) before they actually purchase the home from you. This, of course, begs the question of "Why in the world would I do that?" which we will get into shortly (trust me, there are good reasons).

In a rent-to-own transaction, before your buyer moves in as a renter, you and the buyer would agree on the sale price and other terms. The buyer would pay you a non-refundable option fee, you would both sign paperwork covering the lease, the purchase and the option (which gives the buyer the right to purchase the home at a later date) and hopefully in a year or two the buyer completes the purchase of the home.

I say hopefully because it is important to understand that in a rent-to-own transaction, the buyer is not obligated to purchase your home at the end of the rental period – but if he doesn't he'll be sacrificing his option fee. I'll go into plenty of detail about that later, but understand that the option fee helps motivate the tenant to buy the home.

## Wendy's Wisdom

*A rent-to-own transaction is NOT a guaranteed sale, however, if the tenant-buyer doesn't buy your home; you get to keep their option fee.*

In later chapters we will go into great detail about the entire process. Right now I just want you to have a good foundation of understanding about rent-to-own. Let's recap. A rent-to-own transaction between you (the seller) and a tenant (the buyer) is comprised of:

1) paperwork and contracts,
2) an agreement on price and terms,
3) an option fee,
4) a rental period in which the buyer is renting your home, and
5) the end sale.

So far this probably sounds great for the buyer but mediocre at best for you, the seller. After all, the buyer gets to live in your home and then isn't obligated to buy it at the end of the lease. So that brings us back to the question of "Why in the world would I do that?" Or to put it more bluntly, "What's in it for me?"

### Why Would I Need to do this Rent-To-Own Thing?

In the Introduction I gave you a couple of scenarios that probably hit the mark for you, at least in part. Most of you reading this already have your home up for sale. Those of you who don't have your home up for sale yet are reading this because you know what your market is like and you want to maximize your chances from the beginning. Either way you want to get your home SOLD.

## The Realities of our Current Housing Market – Can You Say "Slump?"

Let's face it, throughout much of the country right now the real estate market is tough for sellers. Many areas went through a period of real estate insanity that will be looked back on as the "Boom Years". The "Boom Years" gave us double digit appreciation rates and home values soared in much of the country. Some areas were so crazy that the appreciation rates were as much as 40% or more in one year. In Miami, Florida, the median selling price of a home in January of 2003 was about $190,000. By January of 2007 the median selling price was $375,000! That's about 100% appreciation in 4 years or 25% per year. How many of you really think that appreciation rates of 25% per year are realistic?

### Wendy's Wisdom

*Not everywhere in the country was seeing such glamorous home price increases. In Southeastern Michigan, where I live, from January 2003 to January of 2007 home values actually DROPPED by 2% (of course it's been much worse since).*

With home prices surging so rapidly, people were buying them like the Nintendo Wii for Christmas. It was a mad rush to buy because if you waited too long they'd be gone. Those fabulous "Boom Years" were great for real estate agents and sellers. A real estate agent could get a listing and start hammering the sign out front. Before they finished, a buyer would drive up and start writing a deposit check, without even looking at the interior. Before that buyer could finish writing the check, another buyer would drive up and start writing a bigger deposit check for more than the asking price. A "for sale" sign attracted buyers like my cats when they hear the can opener.

The simple fact of the matter is the heroic appreciation rates most of you experienced just weren't sustainable. The real estate market in most areas hasn't just settled back down to mere mortal levels, they've dropped below that. Miami, Florida, from January of 2007 to May of 2008 dropped from a median price of $395,000 down to $337,000. By September of 2008, the median selling price dropped to $275,000. That's more than a $100,000 drop in just over a 1 ½ years! And it's still going down as of the writing of this book.

Miami is more of an extreme case than most of the country, both going up and coming down, but it does serve as a good example of how things have changed. Buyers have become scarce, just like my cats when they find out I only opened a can of green beans. Meanwhile, the sellers are popping out everywhere now. It seems like "For Sale" signs on the front lawns are now part of the landscaping that everyone plants when they put in their spring flowers.

*It seems like these signs are everywhere right now*

*These signs are all too scarce*

Unfortunately the "For Sale" signs seem to be lingering well after the spring flowers have wilted. Whether your market is like the plummeting Miami or your local market is much more moderate, odds are it's still much tougher to sell your home now than it was just a couple of years ago. We are facing a housing slump now and it isn't as simple as the fact that buyers are scarce. Even when people want to buy homes, they are finding it much harder to obtain financing. The buyers are facing a "Credit Crunch."

## How the "Credit Crunch" Affects YOU – the Seller

With the severe tightening of the mortgage lending industry, buyers are having a harder time getting mortgages. The subprime mess we've all heard about means many buyers who could qualify for mortgages before are no longer able to.

During the "Boom Years," lenders were putting buyers into adjustable rate mortgages, or ARMs (meaning their interest rate would be increasing after the introductory period, thereby increasing their payment). They did this because the buyer couldn't qualify for a standard mortgage, or even if they could qualify, they couldn't afford the payment because the interest rate on the 30 year fixed mortgage was so much higher. These adjustable rate mortgages are one type of a subprime loan.

The lenders reasoned that it was okay to give buyers these loans because home prices were appreciating so rapidly. The thought was that by the time the new homeowner's mortgage was getting close to adjusting upwards the home would have appreciated enough that the owner could refinance into a conventional fixed rate mortgage.

Unfortunately, the rapid appreciation didn't continue forever and the homeowners discovered that not only could they not refinance their loan into a fixed rate, but they also could not afford the payments when their current loan adjusted upwards. The result of which is the highest number of home foreclosures in our Nation's history.

With so many loans going into foreclosure, a number of smaller lenders went under and some of the larger lenders have stopped writing mortgages altogether. The lenders that continue to provide loans are being much more conservative and have instituted much stricter guidelines, resulting in a "Credit Crunch."

This makes the number of buyers who can qualify for mortgages very small in comparison to the number of homes actually for sale. And to you, the seller, this means that you have a lot of competition when selling your home. The best way to gain an advantage on your competition is to have an edge over them. To get an edge over your competition you could try rent-to-own, or you could set their house on fire or spray paint graffiti all over their siding. You could even be so nasty as to keep pulling their "for sale" sign out of the ground and hide it in your garage. Personally, I would recommend rent-to-own. You are much less likely to spend time

## Wendy's Wisdom

*The "Boom Years" are over and mortgages are scarce now. This is the time to look for alternatives like selling your home on a rent-to-own basis.*

## Can I Possibly Avoid a Foreclosure?

If you are in the difficult situation of falling behind on your mortgage payments and trying to sell your home, offering it on a rent-to-own basis may help you stay out of foreclosure. I wish I could say for certain, because I hate to see people lose their homes to the bank, but obviously it's no guarantee. The last thing lenders want right now is to foreclose on your home. They have gotten pretty flexible in working with homeowners to find solutions. Be sure to include them in the process when trying to find a resolution. As you read on in further chapters, you can evaluate whether you think selling your home as a rent-to-own will help you. Critical factors to consider are:

- *Monthly Payment Adjusting Up?* If your monthly payment has adjusted upwards, will you be able to rent your home to a tenant-buyer for enough to cover the new payment? If not, you will have to cover the difference yourself or get the lender to agree to a reduced payment. There are lenders that will work with you on your interest rate. This is called a *loan modification*. They usually won't change your balance but

6

they might change the interest rate and length of loan. Talk to your lender to discuss your options.

- *Home Prices Dropping?* Do you live in one of the areas where home prices have dropped dramatically? If so, is your home worth much less than your current loan amount? If this is the case you won't be able to sell it to a tenant-buyer for enough to pay off your mortgage. Do you have the extra money to pay off the difference? Do you need to consider foreclosure? Maybe a short sale is your solution versus a rent-to-own. A *short sale* is when you get your mortgage company to accept a lesser amount on the payoff of your mortgage than you owe when you sell your home. This is called "shorting" the mortgage. Many people and lenders have had to consider this alternative with the housing market decline.

- *Behind on Your Payments?* How much are you currently behind in payments? You will need to catch up on this one way or another to stop the foreclosure. The option fee from your tenant-buyer may be enough to cover this. If it isn't, you might be able to use the option fee to cover part of it and then establish a catch up plan with your lender.

Yes, you do have choices to the traditional way of selling your home! Obviously this is the part where I sing the praises of rent-to-own.

## Rent-to-Own, Your Lifesaver in a Drowning Market

I've talked a fair amount about why you NEED to offer your home on a rent-to-own basis to get it sold in this market. But I haven't talked at all about the benefits to you in doing so. After all, most of us hate doing things just because we HAVE to, we would much rather do things we WANT to do.

So here are some of the reasons rent-to-own can be beneficial for you:

1. ***Higher Purchase Price*** - Rent-to-own sales typically command a price premium over traditional sales. The buyer is paying extra for the flexibility he receives by not having to do an outright purchase immediately. I will be going into how to price your house as a rent-to-own in more detail later.

2. ***Higher Rent*** - You may be able to charge more for monthly rent in a rent-to-own than you would for just a straight rental. I will cover this in more detail later.

3. ***Cash Flow*** - If your monthly payments are less than the monthly rent, the difference goes into your pocket.

4. ***Option Fee*** - This upfront fee paid to you by your buyer is what secures the purchase price down the road. If the buyer closes on the home, it would be applied towards the purchase price. If the buyer elects to not purchase the home, the option fee is forfeited and still remains yours. Either way you win. If you were to just rent the home, then the tenant would put down a security deposit. The option fee is different than a security deposit. A security deposit is owned by the tenant and can't be used by the owner, except for repairing damages, unpaid rent and other provisions as mandated under state laws.

## Wendy's Wisdom

*Do you see a trend so far? Rent-to-own sales can make you more money.*

- ***Eliminates the Burden of the Mortgage Payment*** - Hopefully you aren't in this position, but if you are I feel your pain. If you have already moved on to your next home and your old house is sitting empty while you try to sell it, then you are saddled with TWO mortgage payments. Ouch! If the house has been taking a while to sell, you know how fast the money coming out of your pocket adds up. It gobbles up any equity you have at a frightening rate. Placing a rent-to-own buyer that pays that extra mortgage can take away your pain.

- ***Getting Your Home Sold Faster*** - In slow selling markets, offering your home as a rent-to-own can help you get a buyer into the house much faster. This option will open up your pool of buyers significantly.

- **Getting Your Home Sold at All** - If your home is just flat out not selling for whatever reason, offering it as a rent-to-own may be the only way to get it sold.

## Wendy's Wisdom

*Selling your home as a rent-to-own offers a lot of benefits to you: Higher purchase price, cash flow, higher rent, option fee, selling faster and more!*

**My Market isn't Drowning--Is this Still Useful for Me?**

You bet it is! Even if your market is stable or, lucky for you, a "Seller's Market," selling your home on a rent-to-own basis can still be very beneficial. Let's look at a couple of scenarios to understand why.

**Scenario 1 – No Equity**

If you need to sell your home and you have no equity, how do you do it? In other words, you owe as much on your home as it is currently worth. How can you pay the real estate agent a commission and also other closing costs? Sometimes we don't always have the option of waiting until we can afford to sell, even in good markets.

You can try the "For Sale by Owner" route, but even in good markets that tends to have only modest success and, let's face it, is fraught with pitfalls. Selling on a rent-to-own basis can allow you to get a higher purchase price than a conventional sale. This can help give you some room to cover the cost of selling. Plus, having a tenant-buyer in place for a year or two paying your mortgage can help pay down the principal giving you some equity as well.

**Scenario 2 – You've Got to Sell FAST**

It takes time to sell a home, even in good markets. After you have a signed sales contract from a buyer, it can still take anywhere from 30 to 90 days to close. That's at least one more mortgage payment and maybe as many as three more AFTER you have a signed contract.

With the added flexibility of offering your home as a rent-to-own, you can find buyers much quicker. Plus, you can place a tenant-buyer in your home much, MUCH faster than a conventional buyer. Once you have found a rent-to-own buyer for your home, all the time it takes is the screening process (which we'll cover later), signing the paperwork and they can move in. This can be done in just a few DAYS, not months.

**Scenario 3 – Your Home Needs Work**

Selling a home that needs fixing up can be downright difficult. Most buyers (who can get a mortgage) want a home that is in perfect condition. If you can't afford or don't want to fix it up yourself, a handyman rent-to-own buyer can be the perfect solution. The buyer can fix up the house and build some sweat equity during the process. Rent-to-own buyers are not as picky as buyers paying with cash or a mortgage.

You might want to give them the credit for doing the work. For instance, a repair that would cost you $4,000 might be doable by a tenant-buyer themselves for $800 in materials. You can consider giving the buyer a $4,000 credit or a partial credit against the end purchase price. You will need to negotiate this upfront with the tenant-buyer. This creates a win-win situation for both of you, it gets the repair done so you don't have to incur the expense and the tenant-buyer gets some equity in their future home.

I hear sometimes that sellers are concerned about the quality of the tenant-buyer in a fixer-upper rent-to-own home, but I think they can be among the best buyers. The reason is that by doing work in the home themselves, they get a sense of personal investment that the average buyer wouldn't have. In other words, they've taken a house and made it their home. I find that these buyers are more likely to complete the sale at the end of the rental agreement. If you have a concern or it is a large repair, you might want to put into your agreement provisions for licensed and insured workers only, pulling permits for all work, inspections along the way, etc.

**A Special Note About Working with Real Estate Agents**

You might think because you have your home listed with a real estate agent that you can't offer it on a rent-to-own basis. This is the farthest thing from the truth! It works BETTER when your home is listed with an agent.

Not all real estate agents understand how rent-to-own works, but you absolutely can do it. A real estate agent's biggest concern with doing a rent-to-own sale, despite whatever they might tell you, is how they get paid their commission. We'll go over the details of how this works in Chapter 6 – Using a Realtor®. If you need to explain to your real estate agent how rent-to-own works, start with the reassurance that they will still get paid and they'll jump on board. Then give them a copy of this book.

The reason I say it works better when using a real estate agent is they have access to a much larger pool of potential buyers than if you go the "For Sale by Owner" route. Not only that, they can help you avoid numerous pitfalls when it comes to handling necessary documentation and contracts.

11

## When Will Rent-to-Own NOT Work?

While selling your home on a rent-to-own basis is a great solution, it isn't the perfect solution for every situation. There are some times when selling your home as a rent-to-own won't work.

- *You Need Your Equity Out Immediately* - If you need the equity in your home as soon as you sell it, and for some reason wouldn't be able to take out a home equity loan after you place a tenant-buyer, then rent-to-own may not work for you.

Something to keep in mind, however, is whether you really NEED the money from the sale right away or whether you just WANT the money right away. There IS a difference.

If you are in a situation where you are making a monthly payment on that house but are no longer living in it, take a quick look at the numbers. How much is it costing you each month it sits vacant? Then look at the average length of time it takes for homes to sell in your market. Is it 6 months? 9 months? 12 months or more? Then multiply the first by the second and see how much of your equity you are burning through simply because you want to get your home sold to a conventional buyer. Don't forget to include the cost of utilities, too.

- *You are in Foreclosure - and have no way of making up the back payments that are due to the lender.* If the lender isn't willing to agree to some kind of workout solution and won't stop the foreclosure proceedings, this won't work. Note also that even if you bring your payments current, you MUST stay current during your option period with your buyer. If your buyer is paying you and you do not pay your lender, you could be looking at a large lawsuit from your tenant-buyer.

## Wendy's Wisdom

*If you are in a situation where you had to catch up on mortgage payments you should probably get the buyer to write their checks directly to the lender. They can mail them to you and you forward them on, or they can send proof of payments (i.e. if made from their checking they can send you a receipt for payment). You want to make sure you are not tempted to use it for your new home or other bills.*

- *You Can't Provide a Clear Title - when it comes time to sell.* If you can't sell your home conventionally because you can't provide clear title then you can't sell it on a rent-to-own basis either. Although selling on a rent-to-own basis will give you extra time to remove obstructions to conveying the title.

What do I mean by not having a clear title? You may have contractor bills, delinquent property taxes, water and/or sewer charges, etc. that are currently due and have liens placed on your property. These liens will prevent you from selling your home if you don't have enough equity to satisfy all of the debts by the sale of your home. In other words, these bills will get paid from the proceeds of the sale of your home before you get any money. However, if the sale price isn't high enough to cover all debts, you won't be able to convey (transfer) the title to a new buyer.

If you aren't the sole owner of the property all owners must be willing to convey the title. In other words if you've gone through a divorce and your spouse is on title then your spouse must agree and sign off on the transfer. No matter how much of a jerk your spouse might have been during the divorce they, unfortunately, have legal rights. Instead of trying to sell the house out from under them, you are much better off crank calling them at 2 a.m. or signing them up on a bunch of strange mailing lists so they get weird junk mail. It's also the same if you jointly inherited a property. All heirs must agree and sign.

- **You Owe More Than Your Home is Worth** – This does not make a sale impossible, but it can be difficult. If you owe more than your home is worth, do you have the cash to bring to the closing table at the time the tenant-buyer is ready to close? If not, do NOT sell on a rent-to-own; it would be unfair to the tenant-buyer.

If you are able to borrow the money from a family member or friend, do it before you start the rent-to-own with your buyer. Put that extra money right onto your mortgage to pay down the balance so you are ready when the buyer is able to close. Do not wait until the time they are ready to close to borrow the money, it might not be available then. You know how people are, today they say yes, but when you need it they might change their mind or not be able to help you.

- *You Live in the State of Texas* - This is not a joke. Unfortunately, state law in Texas makes it almost impossible to do this type of transaction. Check with a local real estate attorney to see if your situation will allow for a rent-to-own.

If you don't fall into one of the above categories, then you can sell your home on a rent-to-own basis, so read on. In the next chapter we'll get into some of the nitty-gritty details about how rent-to-own works.

# Chapter 2

## How Does Renting-To-Own Work?

**Understanding Rent-to-Own**

In Chapter 1, I was deliberately vague on the details of how the rent-to-own process works so you wouldn't get bogged down in the details. It's time now to get into some of those details so you'll have a deeper understanding. We established that a rent-to-own transaction between a buyer and seller will consist of the contracts, an agreement on price and terms, an option fee, a rental period and the end sale. Let's look at each of those parts now. If you have already decided that this is too much for you, then give this book to your real estate agent. If you need one that understands rent-to-own, please email my office at refer@wendypatton.com so I can refer you to an agent versed in rent-to-own. Let's jump into the details.

**How Rent-to-Own Transactions are Structured – The Contracts**

In any real estate transaction contracts play a vital role. They define the rules of the transaction. In a rent-to-own sale this is no different, although there is a bit more paperwork required to cover the different aspects.

The three contracts needed in a rent-to-own transaction are:

1) Rental Agreement
2) Option Agreement
3) Sales Contract

There is also a *memorandum of option* that I will discuss here in case you decide to use it, but most likely you will not. I will give you a brief overview of each here so that you have a better understanding. We will look at each one individually in great detail in Part 3: Understanding the Paperwork.

## 1) Rental Agreement

The *rental or lease agreement* is very much like the lease agreement used when renting an apartment or home. It defines the term of the lease, dictating how long the renter can live in the property as well as the amount of monthly rent and security deposit.

Additionally, all of the other general rules and conditions of the lease are covered, such as the number of people permitted to live in the property, whether pets are allowed, how many cars, how repairs are handled and so on. I like to include a clause that makes it clear that the renters are not allowed to turn the property into a meth lab or a brothel, just in case they didn't know that. I call it "not using the home for business purposes without approval."

## 2) Option Agreement

The *option agreement* or *option to purchase agreement* gives the tenant-buyer the right to purchase the home from the seller at a later date. It specifies how long the option agreement is valid, in other words, how long the tenant-buyer has to execute the purchase under the current agreement. It does NOT specify the purchase price or terms of the purchase. It does, however, specify the amount of the option fee and whether there is a monthly *option credit*. (Option credits are an agreed upon amount that will be credited against the purchase price should the renter purchase the property as agreed.) The option fee is what makes the option agreement valid however it is not 100% necessary to make it valid. Signing the rental agreement, which is a promise to pay, would also be valuable consideration in most cases. You would rather have them put down a non-refundable option fee since you are the seller.

## 3) Sales Contract

The *sales contract* or *purchase agreement* is the document that covers the details of the actual sale of your house. It includes the purchase price and what non-permanent features of the home are included in the sale, such as the appliances or furnishings or the gorgeous 1965 Mustang convertible in the garage. It specifies how the home is to be paid for at the end of the option time period, either a mortgage or cash sale. Okay, it probably won't be cash so don't get too excited! The sales contract also specifies all of the other terms and conditions of the actual sale, for instance how the property taxes will be prorated, whether the buyer will have a home inspection, etc. In this case, it is a rent-to-own transaction, so the purchase agreement also notes that it is part of the *option to purchase agreement*, thereby binding them together.

## Wendy's Wisdom

*Buyers and sellers can sometimes get very hung up on one particular item in the house. For the buyers, it could be the one thing that really sold them on the house, even though it's not attached, such as a wood burning stove or pool table. For the sellers, it could be the one thing they absolutely want to take with them. It's amazing how intense negotiations can be over this one particular item, sometimes even breaking the deal. We're talking about a house worth a couple of hundred thousand dollars and the buyers and sellers are hung up on an item worth maybe $600!*

*The lesson to learn from this – don't get so caught up in the little stuff that you forget the big picture. You are selling your home, not a life-sized cigar store Indian.*

### Memorandum of Option

The *memorandum of option* is a recordable document that "clouds the title" of the property. In other words, when the memorandum of option is executed by the seller, it may be recorded at the local register of deeds, county recorder's office or whichever government office in your area handles property title work. By recording the memorandum of option it prevents the home from being sold to anyone else (with clear title) while the memorandum is still valid. It does this by preventing the deed or title to the home from being transferred until the memorandum of option is released, this is a form of "clouding the title."

As a seller you usually won't want a memorandum of option. There is usually no advantage to you, and it can cloud your title making it difficult to resell your home if this buyer chooses not to buy.

## How Rent-to-Own Transactions are Structured – The Terms

In addition to the paperwork, which defines the details of the transaction, there are some terms of the agreements that are quite particular to rent-to-own transactions. In addition to being unique, they are extremely important. The terms cover the different financial aspects of the transaction, which can greatly affect the bottom line.

In Chapter 12: Key Points to Negotiate, we will cover how you can negotiate these terms to make the deal better for you. They are:

1. *Monthly Option Credit* – as we mentioned, this would be a portion of the monthly rent which is credited towards the purchase price ONLY if the renter exercises the option to purchase. This credit is in no way mandatory, but can be very helpful to the buyer when it comes time to purchase. As the seller, you want to make sure it is a reasonable amount - don't give too much away! But you also want it beneficial enough to the buyer to entice them to the closing table.

2. *Monthly Rent Amount* – typically rents are priced at market rent or a little bit more on a rent-to-own transaction. However, this amount can always be negotiated to make it better for you.

3. *End Purchase Price* – the amount the buyer will actually pay for the home once they exercise the right to purchase.

This final amount will determine the buyer's new mortgage payments. It will also reflect the net proceeds for the seller. Most rent-to-own sales command a slightly higher purchase price and possibly as much as 5 to 10% more depending on the strength of the real estate market in that area.

4.  ***What is Included in the Sale*** – appliances, furnishings, pool tables and other property all have monetary value. If you include the refrigerator, stove, dishwasher and washer and dryer in the sale you can be adding thousands of dollars worth of value. Don't overlook the value of these items when determining the sale price.

5.  ***Repairs*** – who handles repairs during the rental period? Every repair costs money and it will affect your bottom line, based on who has to pay, especially if the home ends up needing a big ticket item such as a roof or a furnace. This is a point you can negotiate with your tenant-buyer. This will be discussed further later in the book.

6.  ***Closing Costs*** – the costs associated with the sale of the home, such as title insurance, mortgage origination or points, payment to the closing agent, etc. can be quite expensive. It's fairly common to include part of these costs into the mortgage to help reduce the amount of money the buyer has to pay out of pocket at the closing.

7.  ***Home Owner's Association (HOA), Lawn Service, Home Security Systems, etc.*** – monthly and yearly maintenance fees and dues associated with some homes and all condominiums. Other examples of these are pool service, lawn sprinkler maintenance and even country club fees. Many homes won't have these or at least not all of them, but it's obvious that if there are many of these the costs will add up quickly, and should be part of the negotiations.

8.  ***Anything Else Between the Buyer and the Seller*** – that you want to agree on or put into your sales contract. Ideas:

repairs, inspections, occupancy date and time, title insurance, closing costs, etc.

> J. Paul Getty, one of the world's first billionaires, said this about negotiating: "You must never try to make all the money that's in a deal. Let the other fellow make some money too, because if you have a reputation for always making all the money, you won't have many deals."

## An Example

Let's take a look at a sample transaction to help you understand the process. John and Joan Homebuyers were told by their loan officer that they couldn't qualify for a mortgage right now. "Not until you've improved your credit score." They live in a down real estate market and know that now is a good time to buy. They have always dreamed of home ownership. They want a home NOW. They enlist the help of Sally Agent, a local real estate agent, who understands how to do rent-to-own home transactions.

From talking with their loan officer, John and Joan have determined that once they qualify for a mortgage, they can afford the payments on a $220,000 home. So they begin to look in that price range.

Alan and Ashley Homeseller live in the same market. A few months ago Alan received a promotion at work that requires them to relocate to another city. Alan and Ashley know the real estate market is down, but they have no choice but to sell their home now. They have it listed with real estate agent Thomas Broker (and yes, I do go to great lengths to come up with these names).

Alan and Ashley have had their home listed for 4 months at $225,000 without any offers. The need to get their home sold is getting urgent. Their agent, Thomas, recommends Alan and Ashley reduce the asking price to $215,000. He also suggests that they market their home on a rent-to-own basis for $225,000 (Wendy is very impressed with this agent because this agent knows that a rent-to-own is worth more than an outright sale - in almost all cases). After Thomas explains how it works to them, Alan and Ashley agree to add rent-to-own to their listing agreement.

Not long after, Sally Agent shows the house to John and Joan, who decide to make an offer on it. For their initial offer they offer $215,000 for the purchase price, agree to the asking rent amount of $1,500 per month, but ask for a $500 per month option credit. For their option fee, John and Joan offer 1% or $2,150 and a $250 security deposit. They also ask that all appliances in the house (refrigerator, stove, dishwasher, washer and dryer) be included.

After receiving their offer through Thomas, Alan and Ashley make a counter offer of $220,000 for the purchase price, $200 per month option credit and an option fee of 2.5%, or $5,500 with a $750 security deposit. They agree to all of the appliances, except for the refrigerator which is brand new and they want to take it with them.

Getting closer to an agreement, John and Joan counter back, accepting the $220,000 purchase price, but ask for a $350 per month option credit and an option fee of 2%, or $4,400 with a $500 security deposit. They agree to let Alan and Ashley take the refrigerator, but they ask for an 18 month lease and option period instead of 12 months to give them extra time to get their credit in order. (By the way, most tenant-buyers will require 18 months or longer. Very few buyers can repair their credit in less time with the current mortgage climate.)

Happy to finally have buyers for their home, Alan and Ashley accept the last offer. After conducting the proper screening, they agree to sign all of the paperwork and move in within two weeks, giving Alan and Ashley time to move out.

## Wendy's Wisdom

*At this point, it's a good idea to collect a fairly good-sized deposit from the buyers to reserve and secure the property.*

When they meet, they sign the lease agreement, the option agreement, and the purchase agreement. Because the home was built in 1992, the home will not have lead in the paint but they must still sign a *Lead Based Paint Disclosure*[i] (this is Federal law), as well as the seller's disclosure (property condition) form as mandated in their state.

Additionally as part of a smart practice for rentals, they complete a *Property Inventory/Check-in Check-out form (unit condition form)*, which simply details any issues or problems with the home at time of possession.

Here is a breakdown of the money that John and Joan need to bring the day of the paperwork signing:

| | |
|---|---|
| Option Fee - | $4,400 |
| Security Deposit - | $500 |
| First Month's Rent - | $1,500 |
| For a total of = | $6,400 |

Less any deposit already received from the tenant-buyer at the time of initial offer, (recommended for both parties to lock it in).

Once John and Joan sign the paperwork and give the money to Alan and Ashley, they can move in immediately, only 2 weeks after they reached an agreement!

As a side note, in this case the option fee is not enough to pay the entire amount of commission due to the real estate agents up front (which you wouldn't necessarily want to do anyway). Plus Alan and Ashley need some of the option fee to help with their move. They agree to pay the real estate agents 1% of the purchase price up front which is half of the option fee, or ½% to each agent involved and then pay the remaining commissions at the time the house is sold (the closing date). We will talk about why some of the commission is paid upfront to the real estate agents versus paying it all when the home is actually sold in Chapter 6, Using a Realtor®.

## Wendy's Wisdom

*You should document in writing with your real estate agent BEFORE you find a rent-to-own buyer the exact details of how much and when commissions will be paid.*

During the rental period John and Joan take steps to improve their credit score. They didn't have enough money left to buy a new refrigerator, but were able to get financing on one. They were very careful to make all of the payments when due and pay it off in one year. In addition, they paid off two smaller credit cards. They diligently made all utility and other payments on time.

After 15 months in the home John and Joan notify Alan and Ashley that they want to purchase the house. They begin to work with their loan officer and apply for a mortgage. By making on-time payments and paying off debts, their loan officer is able to get them approved.

Now that John and Joan have their loan in place, it's time to complete the sale from Alan and Ashley. You'll recall that Alan and Ashley originally had the home listed for $225,000 but then dropped their asking price to $215,000 for a straight sale or $225,000 for the rent-to-own. They accepted a $220,000 rent-to-own purchase price from John and Joan, with an additional $6,300 in monthly option credits, or a total reduction of $11,300 off their asking price. For the sake of comparison let's say that if they had managed to get a conventional sale on the house, they would accept a reduction of

$10,000 off the $215,000 (= $205,000 selling price). Either way, we'll say that they owe $175,000 for the mortgage on their home. Let's see how they fared at the closing.

*I'm going to get detailed with some numbers here. If numbers bog you down skip them. I summarize them after.*

I'm making a couple of assumptions here:

- ***Transfer/Excise Taxes*** - these taxes vary from state to state, and even sometimes city to city. Many states don't have them at all. I'm using 1 ½% as an estimate which is higher than most areas. They will almost certainly vary a little bit from that where you live.

- ***The Realtor® Commission*** - Commission is also estimated at 6% and can vary by whatever commission amount you set with your agent, they are not fixed.

- ***Closing fees*** - There is also likely to be some additional closing costs charged by the closing agent. They would be the same for each example so I'm going to skip them.

- ***Cash flow*** - Also, in the rent-to-own numbers I'm estimating monthly cash flow based on Alan and Ashley having a monthly mortgage payment of $1350, or $150 per month positive cash flow after receiving $1500 per month in rent.

**Conventional Sale - Asking Price $215,000**

| | |
|---|---|
| Selling Price | $205,000 |
| Realtor® Commission at 6% | - $12,300 |
| Transfer Taxes at 1 ½% | - $3,075 |
| Existing Mortgage Balance | $175,000 |
| Balance due to sellers at closing = | $14,625 |

**Rent-to-Own – Asking Price $225,000**

| | |
|---|---:|
| Selling Price | $220,000 |
| Option Credits | - $6,300 |
| Option Fee | - $4,400 |
| Realtor® Commission at 5% (1% was paid already) | -$11,000 |
| Transfer Taxes at 1 ½% | - $3,300 |
| Existing Mortgage Balance | - $175,000 |
| Balance due to sellers at closing | = $20,000 |
| | |
| Monthly Cash Flow ($150 X 18 months) | + $2,700 |
| Upfront Option Fee less 1% in commission | + $2,200 |
| Total income for sellers = | $24,900 |

As you can see Alan and Ashley actually made over $10,000 more by selling their home on a rent-to-own basis (not bad considering they hadn't gotten any conventional offers anyway).

The critical point in this example is that we have created a win-win-win situation for the tenant-buyers, sellers and real estate agents. It's a win for John and Joan as buyers because they are able to get a rent-to-own home right away when they couldn't qualify for a mortgage. It's a win for Alan and Ashley as sellers because they couldn't get an offer on their home selling it conventionally and in the end they actually made more money from the sale by selling it as a rent-to-own. It was a win for the real estate agent because they got the home SOLD and they got paid their commission!

By creating a win-win-win, everyone walks away happy when the deal is done.

## How to Get Started

In the next section we'll talk about getting started. Reading this book is a great start in the right direction, but you've got to get moving as well. Unfortunately, reading this book isn't enough. You'll have to take the steps to get things going. We are going to go over lots of things in the next section, and you won't be able to do it all at once. I recommend taking it one step at a time. That's the best way. Pick one step out of the next section to get you in action and do it. After you've done that one, pick another and do that. You'll find it's very easy to convert reading this book into action if you break it off into these small and manageable chunks. Take baby steps.

# PART 2:

## PREPARING AND MARKETING YOUR HOME

# Chapter 3

## Repairs - Three Strikes and You're Out!

Before you actually put your home on the market you need to get it ready to sell. If your home is already on the market, well, it's better late than never. Homes in need of repairs and improvements start sending out red flags to buyers as they look. If they see  too many red flags it's out the door and on to the next house. My friend Beth says she thinks there is a "3 strikes and you're out rule."

This means that once the buyer has seen 3 things they don't like or think they have to fix, they move on to the next home. It may not be quite as severe for a rent-to-own buyer, but you still want to think about that. In general, rent-to-own buyers are not as picky as buyers that can get a mortgage. There is an exception to this rule and that is if you are selling your home as a fixer-upper.

When it comes time to sell your home you want to walk a thin line between what to fix and what not to change. You want to get top dollar for your home and get it sold, but at the same time you don't want to sink a ton of money into repairs and improvements using up all of your equity and then some.

If you are using a real estate agent to sell your home, which I do recommend, I suggest you ask your agent to do a walk through with you in the house to point out things that should be fixed and updated. If you do not have a real estate agent, email me at refer@wendypatton.com and I can recommend one in your area. This is a very good place to start. A pair of objective and professional eyes can notice a lot of things that you are used to overlooking because you see it every day. In fact, even if you aren't going to use a real estate agent, I recommend you at least have some objective person experienced in real estate look over your home.

The idea is to get someone that can look at the house through the buyer's eyes. You've been living in the house all this time, so you don't have buyer's eyes. You have homeowner's eyes. Those are the eyes that make you see your house as the best one in the whole neighborhood which should bring in top dollar and have the buyers fighting and clamoring over each other to give you full price offers.

Unfortunately for us, the buyers don't see it that way and they'll pick your home apart piece by piece as they decide whether or not it's good enough for them. That's why we need to take steps to make the house more attractive to our rent-to-own buyers.

## Wendy's Wisdom

*Don't go overboard. I go into lots of detail in this chapter. Focus on the inexpensive and no cost items as your priority. At the end of this chapter I will give you some tips on where you can get materials for free, or very inexpensively, instead of paying full price at the home centers.*

Seller's Eyes                    Buyer's Eyes

I'm going to assume you have a somewhat limited budget for repairs and improvements, because if you had an unlimited budget you wouldn't need this book. You may be reading this and saying, "Oh yeah, my budget is limited, limited to nothing." If that's the case, not to worry, there will be lots of things in both this chapter and the next that you can do for free or for very little money.

I mentioned repairs and improvements. They are definitely separate and distinct and we'll be looking at the value of both. A repair is something like replacing a leaky roof or installing a new water heater, while an improvement is updating a kitchen or painting your front door. You might think that repairs should always come first, but strangely it doesn't always work out that way. Homebuyers are emotional creatures and sometimes the right improvement goes a long way over a needed repair.

Here is an example of a good improvement. A friend of mine had a detached large shed in her yard with a poured concrete floor. It had double doors in the front of the shed. I suggested that she have a garage door installer remove those doors and install a single garage door. The shed was now converted to a garage (much more valuable given the home didn't have a garage before the conversion). This change only cost my friend $850. Now this is a good investment choice.

A real estate agent I know told me a story once that epitomizes how emotional buyers can be. He was acting as a buyer's agent for a young couple looking to buy their first home. They were looking in Ferndale, Michigan, a town that has made a nice comeback in the last decade and is favored by young people as being hip, with lots to offer, but still affordable.

The couple wanted to live close to the downtown area as it has a lot to offer and is a good "walking" downtown. There are some historic homes in Ferndale, built in the 1920s, that can be absolutely beautiful. The agent said he showed them an "Arts and Crafts" style house that was within their budget.

From the outside the house was beautifully designed, very visually interesting, although somewhat worn and in need of repairs. The inside of the house was no better in terms of condition. The living room had shag carpet and glued-on paneled walls with light

31

fixtures straight out of the 1970s. The kitchen also hadn't been updated since the 1970s and was TINY.

The basement utility room was a mechanical nightmare! The wiring was completely hodgepodge with an old 60 amp fuse panel and even some knob and tube wiring. The furnace was an oil burning furnace from the 1940s with the huge oil tank still in the basement. The water lines were lead pipes mixed with galvanized steel. The duct work was wrapped with asbestos. Literally every mechanical aspect of the house was frightening.

On the other side of the basement was a wet bar, an older one with knotty pine panels and quirky light fixtures, but it looked really cool. The couple loved it, especially the husband as he owned a bar. Next to the bar was a bathroom that was tiled completely, floor to ceiling, in this deep, swirly red tile. It was very funky, but the couple absolutely adored it. Based on that old bar and the funky red tile the couple decided they wanted to make an offer on the house.

The agent did everything he could to talk them out of it. The house was a mechanical nightmare. Almost the entire rest of the house needed updating. And the total cost for the repairs, he knew, was going to be WAY beyond their budget. The couple persisted and wanted to make an offer. The other crazy thing about this house was that it was priced at market value as if none of those repairs and updates needed to be made (yes, the listing agent overlooked a few details in the remarks about the condition). The couple still wanted to make an offer.

They put together the offer and their agent submitted it for them. He got a call back from the listing agent saying that she had another offer as well and the seller wouldn't take anything less than full asking price with no concessions. My friend was flabbergasted. Mind you, this is in Michigan, at a time when the market was definitely a buyer's market. He told the other agent that the house needed a tremendous amount of repairs and was already priced at retail value. He didn't understand how anyone in their right mind would pay full price for that home, but the listing agent persisted, saying, "Full price offers only."

Well, the agent went back to his buyers and told them their initial offer had been rejected and that if they wanted the house they would have to offer full price with no concessions. Fortunately his buyers finally decided that full price was too much to pay for that house so they continued looking.

As a side note, the story does have a happy ending. The couple ended up picking a house that was just as close to downtown Ferndale as the other, was bigger in size, in MUCH better shape, and at a lower price.

## Wendy's Wisdom

*Tenant-buyers will notice everything wrong with your home because they will be living in it before buying it, therefore, you will want to make sure all repair items, and who will be paying for them, are covered in the contract.*

Let's take a walk through your home to see what kind of repairs and updates you might want to make. We'll start outside because that's what the buyers see first. This is where they decide if they will even go inside your home.

## Outside

The important thing about the outside of your house is that it needs to have curb appeal. Have you seen the TV show on the DIY Network called *Desperate Landscapes*? Does your house qualify? Hopefully not. Take an objective look at the exterior and landscaping of your home, odds are, unless it's show quality, there are probably some areas that could stand some improvement.

## *Roof*

Roofs get a lot of attention from buyers, but usually only if it is in dire straits. If your roof has shingles falling off and crumbling, or even worse heaving from the underlayment due to moisture in the attic that is a HUGE red flag that's going to scare away many buyers. Replacing a roof can be moderately expensive to downright costly depending on your roof layout and the type of materials.

Patch jobs on roofs stand out worse than just having an old roof. I don't recommend patching because that projects to the buyers that you are only doing the bare minimum to take care of the house. They will already have a biased opinion before they even set foot inside. IF they even set foot inside.

If your roof is in moderate shape or even older, but still functional without looking horrible, I don't recommend replacing it. There are other areas in the house where the money can be better spent.

If your roof is the eyesore of the neighborhood or even just the eyesore of your home it's time to replace it. If you can't afford to have it done you might want to work a deal with the rent-to-own buyer where their option fee helps pay for the new roof, or you can extend an option credit to them for the repair, plus some additional option credit. Let's say a new roof costs $3,000 to have it replaced professionally. You might give your tenant-buyer an option credit of $3,000 or more if they do it themselves. Many buyers would like to do this if they are handy. This works both ways, if they buy the house they get a new roof and you didn't have to pay for it. If for some reason they don't buy, then you get a new roof, which makes reselling much easier, and you didn't have to pay for it.

Either way, you don't have to pay for it, which keeps your money where it belongs - in your pockets.

## Landscaping

### *Flowers, Pruning, and Mulch*

When it comes to landscaping you can spend just a hundred dollars to freshen things up or you can spend tens of thousands of dollars to put in pavers and a huge deck and so forth. I don't recommend spending too much. To get the most bang for the buck out of landscaping I recommend putting in lots of fresh flowers (assuming it is warm where you live), pulling out all the weeds and trimming everything that's overgrown. Cut back and spruce it up! Then mulch it, mulch it, mulch it. Mulch is a great solution for sprucing up a tired landscape. It's inexpensive and makes things look fresh and new.

### *Decks*

If you have an existing deck that is completely falling apart, get rid of it but don't put a new one in, unless you can afford it. If you take out an existing deck, turn that space into flowerbeds or make sure grass is planted and growing. If you have a deck that is in disrepair see if you can fix it up and put a new finish on it. The most inexpensive way to make your old deck look new is to borrow a power washer to clean it and then put a fresh coat of stain or finish on the deck. It's very inexpensive and is something you can do in a day.

A really nice touch for your yard is to have a functional outdoor living space. These are fancy words for making sure your yard is both usable and accessible. Buyers don't just want a yard to look at, they want a yard to use. A great (and inexpensive) way to do this is to make sure you have a small table with a couple of chairs outside. Put them on your deck, if you have one. If you don't have a deck, find a nice space in your yard for them. If you don't have a set like this, don't go out and buy one. See if you know someone you can borrow them from until you sell your home.

## *Siding*

What kind of finish does your home have? Is it brick, stucco, vinyl or aluminum siding? A good bet to clean up the face of your home no matter what kind of siding it has is to power wash. Get rid of the dirt and debris, and that will help freshen up the look of your house. If you don't own a power washer, borrow one. If you can't borrow one you can rent one for a day from your local hardware company.

Brick homes can be very low maintenance until the mortar starts crumbling and then you'll need to have it repaired. A good mason can tint their mortar to match your home's existing mortar. That way you'll only have to repair the areas that need it, instead of the entire house.

If your stucco is crumbling or has large cracks, you'll want to get those areas repaired. If you can get an exact match on the finish of the repairs, great. Otherwise you'll want to paint it all so you have an even finish. The cost of the paint is all you will have if you paint it yourself.

Vinyl and aluminum siding are pretty easy to work with. If you have damage you can just replace those pieces, quite reasonably. The trick however, is that even if you get the exact same color the siding originally was, it won't be the same as your existing siding that's on the house. The sun fades the siding color over the years. Fortunately siding can be painted.

## *Windows*

Replacing a house full of old windows can be so expensive you'll feel like you are passing a kidney stone. Brand new windows don't stand out that well above existing windows made to look new.

If you have any broken windows, they should be fixed. In most cases, either with single pane or double pane windows the glass itself can just be replaced without replacing the whole window frame, which makes it much cheaper.

## Wendy's Wisdom

*Here is a trick for siding when it comes to painting. If you are only repairing or replacing on one or two sides of the house you can just paint those sides. Take a piece of the existing finish to your local home center or paint store and they can do a color match. It won't come out 100% exactly right if you look at it through a microscope, but if it's painted on an entire side of a home it will be so close you won't be able to tell the difference from one side of the house to another. This way the house looks great and it saves you a lot of effort. Also, another trick, to replace a piece of siding that has faded, replace it using a piece hidden by a tree or on a side that people won't notice as much as the front or back where it is needed. Put the new, brighter piece in more hidden spot.*

If you have old single pane windows, make sure the glazing is fresh. If it is crumbling or missing in areas, scrape the old glazing off and apply new. Don't put new glazing over the old glazing because it won't stay on. You can spread glazing with a caulk gun and a putty knife. The glazing itself is only a few dollars a tube. The cost is mostly in labor, but it's easy enough to do yourself.

If you have double pane windows that are fogged because of damaged seals you'll want to think about replacing the glass, because buyers really notice the fogging. Check to see if you have a warranty from your manufacturer, which could definitely save you some money.

Make sure the windows look new, even if they are a hundred years old. Clean the frames up and paint them white. A quart of paint and a brush should cost you less than $15, but are well worth it for the results. You'll want to get an exterior grade paint or similar that can handle temperature changes and condensation, particularly if you live in an area with harsh winters. Never paint windows closed, if you do they can't open once dry.

The other thing to keep in mind with windows is whether the balancers are broken. In other words, do you have to prop your window open with a stick? If so, the balancers are broken. This is something that happens with older windows. Typically these can be replaced without replacing the whole window. It's much less expensive to do it that way.

Buyers rarely notice this problem unless you have the windows propped open when they view the home, but since you are selling on a rent-to-own basis, they will certainly notice while they are living there. Instead of spending the money to replace them you may just want to offer a credit for repairing them, if the buyers complain.

### *Driveway*

A crumbling, crack-filled or heaved driveway can ruin the curb appeal of a home, even when everything else is gorgeous. I know, I know. It's hard to understand how buyers can be so picky about something like that. After all, the driveway hasn't blown out any tires recently.  Unfortunately, tearing out and replacing an existing driveway can be very costly.

Heaved slabs of concrete sometimes can be leveled out by a company that drills holes into the concrete and then pumps pressurized concrete into the holes to level the whole slab out. This is less expensive than replacing the whole slab. If the concrete is crumbling or cracked it can be repaired if the condition isn't too bad.

Once any repairs are done, it's a good idea to have the whole thing top coated. This is a great way to give an old driveway new life. Another option is to have the driveway covered with asphalt. This will depend on your neighborhood. In some areas asphalt driveways are quite common while in others they are very rare and stand out as a cheap fix.

## Wendy's Wisdom

*Before we go inside this is a good place to remind you that you are selling your home as a rent-to-own. Buyers will be less picky than regular retail buyers. Things that are in mediocre condition on a rent-to-own home are best just cleaned up and made presentable, not replaced. Remember, focus on the free or nearly free things to get the maximum effect for the least amount of money.*

## Inside

Now that we've tackled the outside, let's move inside and see where you can get the most out of your money.

### *Entryway*

No matter how you enter your home, through an entryway into a living room, a foyer, or a mudroom, it must be nice. It is the first impression someone walking into your home receives.

The front door is the first part of the entryway and it's no place to ignore. Give it a fresh coat of paint and make sure the molding is in excellent condition.

There shouldn't be any holes in the walls or the ceiling. No dents from doorknobs hitting the walls. If the walls have glued-on paneling left over from the 70s or 80s, it's time to take it off and skim coat the drywall or plaster to get a smooth finish. Follow that up with a fresh coat of paint.

### *Flooring*

Now, take a look at your floor. Be honest with yourself. How does it look? Is it stained, chipped, torn or just plain ugly? Is it outdated? If you have carpet and the condition isn't too bad, rent a cleaner to bring back its glory.

## Hardwood

If you've got hardwood, that's great. People love hardwood floors. If the finish is worn but the floor is in pretty good shape, I recommend first putting down an area rug to cover the bad spots. If an area rug won't do the trick, you can rent a floor sander (the random orbit kind) from your local home center and strip the finish off and apply fresh coats of stain and polyurethane. Unless you have experience refinishing floors, I absolutely do NOT recommend renting a drum floor sander to strip and smooth the floors. These suckers take an experienced touch and if you try it on your own you will most likely gouge at least one divot into your floor. If your hardwood floor needs that kind of refinishing, hire a professional or offer a credit to the tenant-buyers.

## Ceramic Tile

If you've got ceramic tile, you want to think about how it will look to a buyer. Trends in ceramic tile change. If the tile itself is pretty neutral but the grout is old and in an old style you might want to think about having the grout removed and redone, or at least have the grout pressure steam cleaned. If the ceramic is too beat up it can be removed.

## Vinyl or Linoleum Flooring

Okay, here's the thing about vinyl and linoleum. In lower cost houses it makes for a fine flooring surface. In mid-range and higher end houses buyers don't like to see linoleum. The range will depend on your area. I've seen $250,000 and up homes in the Midwest where buyers like to see better floors, but I've also seen $500,000 homes on the West Coast where vinyl is perfectly acceptable.

If you already have vinyl or linoleum in your home that is not outdated and in good shape I wouldn't replace it unless you have a high-end home (leave it be in mid-range homes). If your vinyl or linoleum is outdated or worn, I wouldn't replace it with more of the same unless you have a lower priced home. Whatever you do, I don't recommend the adhesive-backed squares of vinyl -- use sheet vinyl instead. I have yet to see a quality installation job with those adhesive-backed squares.

### Wood Laminates

I love wood laminates. They are very durable and look fantastic. The best part is that they are very affordable. I have seen wood laminates for as little as .99 cents a square foot. The second best part about wood laminates is that they are incredibly easy to install. As far as flooring goes wood laminates are the easiest for the do-it-yourselfer. You can install them right over your old floor surface, like linoleum and out-dated tile as long as its level (just make sure you put down the proper underlayment). Plus it's a project that can easily be done in one day. Go to one of the home improvement stores for instructions or a short class.

### Living Rooms, Family Rooms, Dining Rooms and Bedrooms

These rooms are all essentially boxes and are very easy to do repairs and updates in. Like the entryway, all of the walls should be hole free and get a fresh coat of paint, if the paint is out of date. All of the flooring guidelines I talked about above apply here as well.

If you have wallpaper on the walls, as long as it is in good shape and not too gaudy leave it there. Old, ugly wallpaper can easily be removed (usually) with a steamer or wallpaper adhesive solvent and then the walls can be repainted. Get an opinion (someone that will be very honest with you) about your wallpaper. Is it outdated? Is it ugly? Or is it neutral? Get rid of borders, they date your home to the 80's. Most buyers will not like your wallpaper.

A note here about paint colors. Neutral is best. When you are living in a house it's okay to paint it whatever colors suit you, but when it's time to sell you need to go with neutral or trendy colors. Also, white is not the best color choice. Your local paint store or

41

your real estate agent can help you select good neutral colors. Ask them what is really in right now.

If you have a fireplace, that's great. Most buyers love them. As long as the hearth and surround for the fireplace are functional and not falling apart, I wouldn't do much to them. Just make sure the fireplace is clean.

### Light Fixtures

Light fixtures are a great improvement to make. Brand new fixtures can really improve the appearance of a room. Especially light fixtures with ceiling fans. Changing out fixtures is easy to do and quite affordable. I don't recommend putting in the cheapest fixtures you can find, because they look cheap - especially cheap ceiling fans. However, I also strongly advise against spending a lot of money on super fancy lights

*Don't spend too much on lights, but don't go this cheap.*

The one fixture I do recommend spending just a little bit more on is the dining room chandelier. Those tend to be the center piece of the dining room so you want them to stand out and draw positive attention.

### Master Bedroom

I'm covering this one separately from the other bedrooms because it's more important. This is the room where your rent-to-own buyers will be sleeping. We want the master bedroom to be better than the other bedrooms. All of the rules about the walls, the flooring and the light fixtures apply here too. If you are on a really tight budget and you have to choose between painting other bedrooms, putting new light fixtures in other bedrooms or changing the flooring in other bedrooms versus the master bedroom, you want to give the master bedroom top priority.

If your master bedroom already has a nice ceiling fan in it and you buy a new ceiling fan for another bedroom that's nicer, it's worth it to swap them out. Put the one that's currently in your master bedroom into the other bedroom and put the better one in your master bedroom.

### *Doors*

This is also a good time to talk about doors, both entry doors into rooms and closet doors. Unless a door has got big holes in it, you can make it look brand new with a fresh coat of semi-gloss white paint. Yes, I know I said before that white wasn't a good choice, but that was for the walls. For doors, molding, baseboards and other trim, white is good. If you've got solid wood doors that swell and shrink with weather changes and then stick when you try to open and shut them, it's time to get out the hand planer. This is a no-cost fix that keeps buyers from having a negative impression every time they go into a room. Shave off the area that is rubbing on the door trim.

When you paint a door spend the extra five minutes to take it off its hinges and remove the doorknob. Hinges and doorknobs that have paint on them just don't look good. Buyers will notice, and all of the benefit you would have gained from the freshly painted door is wiped out by the ugly, painted hardware. Also, if you've already taken the time to take the door hardware off this is an excellent time to replace them if they are old and ugly. New hinges and a new doorknob are dirt cheap – around ten dollars combined – and make a wonderful impression on buyers.

The last rooms in the house we haven't covered yet are the kitchen and baths. I was saving them for last because they are the most important. They are also, by far, the most expensive to update and repair, but there are some tricks to maximizing your repairs and improvements in these rooms to try to keep the budget modest.

## Bathrooms

I'm going to split bathrooms into two categories. The first is *passable* and *nice*. The second is *falling apart* and *ugly*. In the first category the nice part is pretty obvious. If your bathroom was updated recently with a new tub, new toilet, new sink and vanity, etc. I'm calling it *nice*. This type of bathroom probably needs very little work, just make sure the walls and floors are in good shape as well.

 *Passable*, is a bathroom that hasn't been updated too recently but has a white tub, a decent white toilet, and a neutral vanity and sink. If the colors aren't white but are neutral colors this is okay too. Passable bathrooms can be saved with little effort. If the tub has chips in the finish, you can touch it up with glazing or if it's too beat up have the entire tub reglazed. A professional can do this for approximately $300-$400. Many will guarantee the results for a period of time.

 Toilets are pretty easy. Either they work or they don't. If it's in between those, where it works right if you jiggle the handle or have to take the lid off the tank and fiddle with some doohickey, then fix it. Toilet repair kits are both inexpensive and easy to install. The thing about toilets is that if it doesn't work or it leaks, the parts to fix it are not expensive. As a side note, unless the toilet seat is brand new or looks brand new, you should replace it. A new toilet seat costs about ten dollars and is well worth the investment.

 Next comes the sink and vanity. If the vanity cabinet is ugly but still functional you can give it a new finish with a fresh coat of white high-gloss/enamel paint. If the sink and vanity top are outdated consider replacing them. You can put in a new cultured marble vanity top for less than a hundred dollars. In fact, if you want to splurge you can replace the whole sink and vanity for less than two hundred in most cases. In fact, you can do it for even less if you follow my tips for getting inexpensive and free materials at the end of this chapter.

 Faucets and shower fixtures are a great upgrade to make. If your bathroom is passable these can go a long way towards making them look updated. You can get a new faucet for about $40 to $50 and a new shower fixture from $40 to $80. Don't over do it with these, but don't go cheap either. Something with a modest flare is a good way to go. Remember if you don't sell your home soon, you will have to live with the old ones falling apart, anyway.

*Just make sure you turn the water off first!*

It's also important to make sure the walls are in good shape, without holes. Remember, spackle is our friend and a fresh coat of paint goes a long way. When it comes to floors in the bathrooms, carpet is not a good choice. You want something moisture resistant. Tile or sheet vinyl are the best choices, followed up by either wood laminate or engineered hardwood. Wood laminate and engineered hardwood are water resistant but cannot handle standing water. They'll swell up and will be ruined. I also don't recommend true hardwood because water can cause both swelling and wood rot.

What if your bathroom is downright ugly or is a barely functional? You've got a couple of choices when your bathtub and toilet are sky blue or mud brown or any other of a rainbow of colors that just scream "dated". You can replace them, which is the best choice but also the most costly. You can replace the toilet (not too expensive) and reglaze the tub.

Replacing the tub, toilet, sink and vanity can be done for anywhere from $1500 to $2000. This is definitely the most costly improvement we've talked about so far, outside of replacing the roof. The other option is to cover up the tub with a new liner, although some companies charge more for this than just replacing the tub, but it is a lot less mess and time. You can also have the tub reglazed to a white or beige finish. This is cheaper and an effective solution. The tub is often the most intimidating part about updating a bathroom. Replacing a toilet and sink and vanity combined can be done for about $500. But what do you do about the tub?

If you have the money I strongly recommend replacing the bath fixtures if your bathroom is sending the buyers running. In the end it will be well worth it when attracting your rent-to-own buyers. Think about what it costs you each month to make the mortgage payment. If updating the bathroom is the difference between a few more months of not being able to sell, versus finding a rent-to-own buyer right away then the decision becomes quite clear.

However, if you simply don't have the money, you can always offer your tenant-buyer a credit for making the update themselves. If it would cost them $2,000 to get the updates done you might offer a $3,000 or $3,500 credit, giving them some sweat equity for their investment.

## Wendy's Wisdom

*We don't always have funds available to do all of the updates we would like, and that's okay. If you are willing to work with your rent-to-own buyer, you can reach an agreement that works well for everyone.*

### Kitchen

The kitchen is probably the single-most important room of the house. Not every buyer feels this way but the majority does. The better the kitchen is the more forgiving a buyer will be with other faults in the house. Doing a complete kitchen remodel is enough to break the bank of just about any home seller. Most of the time it isn't necessary.

The three biggest expenses in updating a kitchen are the cabinets, counters and appliances. The only time I would recommend replacing the cabinets is if the existing ones are completely falling apart, which is very rare. If your cabinets are just plain ugly and outdated your best bet is to paint them with white (or brown), high gloss/enamel paint. Then replace the hardware, both the knobs and the hinges. Stainless steel is a good bet for knobs and hinges, if it matches your faucet. This will make your cabinets look brand new. The paint will cost around $50 and the hardware the same. Don't spend a ridiculous amount of money on fancy hardware.

After making the cabinets look brand new, we need to look at the countertops, are they salvageable? If they are passable, keep them.

You've got a few choices when it comes to replacing the counter top: laminate, tile, man-made stone, granite, and other natural stone. Laminate is the cheapest and can look really nice. Tile is nice, but not so in favor right now. Granite is probably the most popular right now, but can also cost an arm and a leg. On high end homes laminate counters come across as cheap. Buyers for this price range of homes expect more.

The cost of replacing counters really depends on the size of your kitchen. If you have a smaller kitchen with limited counter space you can replace the counters for just a couple of hundred dollars if you put in laminate, using an in-stock counter, but the prices just go up and up from there. If you can afford it I recommend replacing an ugly or damaged countertop. Just replacing the countertop and repainting the cabinets can make an ugly, outdated kitchen look new and it can be done for around $500. If your kitchen is larger and you need a custom laminate it could be up to $1,500.

The appliances are something else entirely. If you still have harvest gold or avocado green appliances, which thankfully are getting to be fewer and fewer, it's better to just take them out and sell your home without them. An otherwise beautiful kitchen will be marred horribly by these old ugly appliances. It's like looking directly at the sun, the buyer won't be able to see anything else for a while just a burned imprint of a harvest gold refrigerator. Just get rid of them. You can buy almost new, neutral appliances at a used appliance store.

Flooring in the kitchen, like the bathrooms, should be water resistant, although hardwood in the kitchen is more acceptable than in the bathroom, if you already have it. If you can only update the floors in just one room of your house I recommend the kitchen.

Don't skimp on the walls either. Like every other room, make sure there aren't any holes. But this is also the best room for a new coat of paint with a neutral color.

Ok, we've gone through your entire house now and looked at every room. Hopefully you've gotten some ideas about what you can do to make your home more appealing to buyers. As a reminder it's a good idea to have some objective eyes look at your home with you to help you see the things you are used to overlooking.

## Wendy's Wisdom

*Odds are you won't be able to or won't need to do everything we've covered. The important thing to take away from this chapter is to really focus on the things that need to be done and the things that can be done most inexpensively.*

Some of the repairs and improvements were fairly costly, but in most rooms cleaning up the walls and a simple paint job can really help make the room look better. Paint and spackle are pretty darn inexpensive when you think about it. By economizing your repairs and improvements, you'll get the most bang for your buck and still make your home more appealing to rent-to-own buyers.

## What to Do if You Have NO Money for Repairs

If your repair budget is zero, it's all about the elbow grease and working with your tenant-buyers. The first thing to do is to roll up your sleeves and start doing what you can around the house without having to spend money. You'll be surprised how much nicer you can make your home look by just putting the effort in. De-clutter and get rid of the extra junk or items in your home that you don't need any longer. Get them out of your home. Get junk out of closets and off of the surface of furniture and counters. If you are a packrat and can't live without your junk, then pack it up and move it to a storage unit or a friend's home that really loves you. No one else will appreciate your collectibles like you do. De-clutter, de-clutter, de-clutter whether you have money or you don't.

Also, look around your house for materials you already have. Leftover paint cans are good for touching up paint in rooms, when you can't repaint the whole room. Old pieces of molding or trim can be used to replace damaged ones. Leftover siding can be used to fix damaged areas on the exterior. Most of us tend to store our old stuff thinking we might need it at some point or other. Well, now is the time to dig through the garage, basement and attic and find out what you still have to fix up your home.

Another great source for free materials for your home is www.Craigslist.org and www.Freecycle.org. www.Craigslist.org has a section for free items, while everything on www.Freecycle.org must be free. With a zero dollar budget free opportunities are a great way to make improvements. I just looked on www.Craigslist.org for my area and saw someone giving away doors, wall sconces, paint and sheets of drywall. This was three different people and it was all today!

Additionally www.Craigslist.org is a great place to get low cost materials, too. You can find kitchen cabinets, bathroom vanities, ceramic tile, wood flooring, doors, windows and on and on. Check other local groups or community bulletin boards for materials as well.

## What if You Can't Do Work Yourself?

Let's say your home needs repairs, you have no money and you are unable to do the work yourself. You can offer your home as a handyman special. Let the tenant-buyer do the work and reap the rewards. You can give them an "option credit" for doing the work themselves. Rent-to-own buyers love this because it gives them equity in their home and also gives them pride of ownership that makes them want to buy the home at the end of the rental period.

There are certain improvements the tenant-buyers can do on their own. But others are ones you want to have a licensed contractor perform to make sure they are done right (sometimes you'll get lucky and your tenant-buyer will be a licensed contractor). You'll also want to work with your tenant-buyer to make sure any necessary permits are pulled and the final inspections are performed. This protects you and the tenant-buyer.

It's particularly important for you to have permits pulled and licensed contractors perform work. If the rent-to-own buyer doesn't close on the house and you get it back, then you know the work was done right.

## Home Warranties

Once you place a tenant-buyer into your home it's a very good idea to obtain a home warranty. This offers a measure of repair protection for both you and the tenant-buyer.

If you aren't familiar with home warranties, they are different from home insurance. They typically cover many repairs and replacements on things that insurance would not cover. Appliances, furnaces, water heaters, air conditioners are just a few of the things a home warranty covers.

While my contracts stipulate that repairs are the responsibility of the buyer (which I'll cover later in Part 3), home warranties are great protection from having repairs be budget busters. If a tenant-buyer is hit with a hefty repair bill during the rental period they may not be able to afford it. If they can't pay, you would have to. What if you can't afford it? This is why a home warranty is great protection for the tenant-buyer and you.

Talk with your real estate agent about home warranties. They will be able to give you details and help you sign up.

In the next chapter we'll take a look at what to do after the repairs and improvements to really get your home ready to sell and stand out from the crowd. It's called *staging*, and all too often it's a crucial part of home selling that is ignored by most sellers.

# Chapter 4

## Curb Appeal and Home Staging

## Getting the Most
## Bling for the Buck

**Emotions Rule the Game**

When it comes to selling your home you want it to really appeal to buyers in a positive way. You want buyers to love your home, to look around and go, "Ooh, look at that," or "Wow, that's beautiful." Your home should have some pizzazz, some sizzle. In other words you want to trick your home out and give it some bling!

*Staging* is when your home is decorated and arranged nicely or "staged" as if Martha Stewart was living there, but really isn't. You can stage your home if you are still living there, or you can stage it if you have already moved out.

Home staging can be done professionally or you can do it yourself.

This will help you get your home sold and help you get the highest price for your home. Properly staging a home will set in the buyers mind how beautiful the home can be and show how much potential it has.

**"You never get a second chance to make a first impression!"**

## Wendy's Wisdom

*Staging is a good idea when you are selling, even if you are selling your home as a fixer-upper. Helping buyers see the potential your home has will encourage them to buy.*

One of the great things about staging your home is that it can be done with little to no money. No matter what your budget is, even if it is zero you can do some staging techniques to increase the appeal of your home.

Well-staged homes that are competitively priced consistently outsell non-staged homes, even the fixer uppers. It's a strange phenomenon, but like I said in the last chapter, buyers are emotional creatures, even to the point that they sometimes choose a lesser, but well-staged home over a better-but empty or non-staged home.

The following story illustrates this perfectly -

Another real estate agent I know told me that he was showing rental homes to a couple with 5 kids. They were looking for a newer home with at least 4 bedrooms, a basement, a 2 car garage and a short commute time.

There were several homes to choose from in their price range. The first one was a builder's model. It had never been lived in. It was completely empty with no furnishings, but the appliances were included. This home had seen numerous walk-throughs and the carpet was a little dirty, the landscaping wasn't in very good shape and the basement floor had many hairline cracks in the concrete. In short, despite being brand new, the home didn't show very well and had the highest rental rate. However, it was very large in size, met all of their needs, and had a short commute time.

The second home was about 5 years old, and was almost the same size as the builder's model. It had a ton of built in storage in the garage, as well as a very smooth floor plan. As a bonus, it had a fifth room in the basement that could be used as a bedroom, which gave all of the kids their own rooms. Unfortunately, this home didn't show all that well either. The owners were in the process of moving out, so there were only odds and ends strewn about the home and there were two pipes dripping in the basement over the laundry area. The rental rate was $100 per month less than the builder's model and the commute time was just as short.

The third home was the smallest. It still had the 4 bedrooms, garage and basement, but was clearly smaller than the other two and was about 10 years old. It was also the farthest away, adding about 15 minutes commuting time each way. The rental rate was $25 per month more than the second home, even though the neighborhood wasn't any better. This home was beautifully staged, however. All of the furnishings were present and were well laid out. The dining room table was set with fine china. The master bedroom had a nicely coordinated bedroom set. None of the furnishings were included with the rental, but it gave the family a chance to visualize living in the home and picture in their mind where they would put their own things.

Guess which house the couple chose? You guessed it, the third one. Despite the fact that it was the farthest away and the smallest home they liked what they saw and felt. If you took away all of the home staging that had been done there was absolutely nothing about this home that was better than the other two. In fact, it was inferior in pretty much every way, but it LOOKED GOOD! Many people can't visualize what a home would look like furnished when it is vacant. Staging, or partially staging, is critical for many buyers to make a buying decision.

As I said, buyers are emotional creatures and we need to appeal to their senses to draw in their positive emotions. We have five senses: sight, touch, taste, smell and sound. We want to appeal to our tenant-buyers on as many levels as possible. You might think when someone walks through a home you can appeal only to one sense, sight. But this isn't true. You can actually appeal to all of the senses. As in the last chapter, we are going to walk through your home to look at how you can stage your home to attract buyers. We'll start outside again.

## Wendy's Wisdom

*I go into a lot of detail here. Don't try to do every single thing here or you'll feel overwhelmed. Just focus on the things that work best for you and are most affordable for you. Remember, you are selling your home as a rent-to-own, so your buyers most likely won't be as picky.*

# Home Staging – Doing It Yourself

### Outside

It's all about the *curb appeal* outside your home. The reason it's called *curb appeal* is that when the potential buyers pull up in their cars alongside the *curb* and look at the home through their windows, it needs to be *appealing*. If a home doesn't have any curb appeal many buyers won't even bother to get out of the car, they just go on to the next one. So curb appeal is designed to get the buyers out of the car, give them a favorable impression and then get them inside the house.

## Wendy's Wisdom

*Remember the rule of 3 strikes and your home is out? Well, if your home has too many strikes when viewed from the curb you are already out.*

No matter how beautiful your home might be on the inside, if it doesn't have curb appeal too, you won't get the buyers inside to look at it. And the buyers you do get inside will be biased because in their minds is how ugly the home looked from the outside.

Fortunately curb appeal is mostly about elbow grease, getting outside and getting your hands dirty.

### Weeds, Weeds, Weeds

When you are selling your home there is absolutely no reason you should have weeds anywhere in your yard. Pull 'em out, spray 'em dead, do whatever it takes but make sure you don't have any weeds. The annoying thing about weeds is that they keep coming back. Unlike the beautiful flowers and gardens we plant that we struggle to keep alive and looking lovely, weeds know they are ugly so they have an incredible survival instinct. As long as your home is on the market you'll need to stay on top of those pesky weeds. Do not forget that mulch we talked about before. It will help keep down those weeds as well.

Your lawn should be mowed neatly and regularly. People like to see those nice even, symmetrical cut lines from lawn mowers. It shows that taking care of your lawn is something you take pride in, not the all-to-infrequently performed chore that you hate to do. Mow the grass regularly and keep it mowed as long as the house is on the market.

You should also make use of an edger - one of those doohickeys that create a nice border between your lawn, driveway and sidewalks. A trimmed edge is much more appealing than grass that has spilled over onto the concrete and is slowly trying to take it over. If you don't have an edger borrow one from that neighbor whose lawn looks like it could be a manicured golf course. I guarantee he has one. While your home is on the market it's also a good idea to keep your lawn fertilized and well watered. This not only helps cut down on the weeds, but it also keeps your lawn nice and green and healthy.

If you happen to live in the southwest where water is scarce, you might not have grass but have a rock yard. If you live in an area where lawns aren't part of the normal landscaping, then whatever you have for a yard make sure it's neat and weeded. If your yard consists of rocks, spray them off with a hose before showings to get all of the dust off. Get some fancy rocks and place them here and there so they look nice and take the monotony out of a broad expanse of plain rocks.

So far these suggestions have cost pretty much zero dollars and will go a long way towards making the outside of your home look nicer. Remember, even if you are going to sell your home as a fixer upper, it's still a good idea to take whatever steps you can towards making your home look nice. Not only will it help you find that fixer-upper tenant-buyer but it will also help you get the best price for your home.

### *Shrubs, Flowers and More Flowers*

Now it's time to spend a little bit of money to really make your landscaping look fabulous, but before you go shopping, any existing shrubs and trees you have should be well pruned. If they are too overgrown to look good after pruning, yank them out and put new ones in.

When it comes to planting shrubs you want to go with a good blend. They should be affordable, but also look good. In other words don't buy the cheapest, tiniest shrubs you can find because they'll be too small and you don't have time for them to grow out – you are trying to sell your home *now*.

Additionally, it's a good idea to plant shrubs that stay green year round. That way if you are selling in a season when most things have lost their leaves, you still have nice green landscaping. Good choices are holly, rhododendrons, and evergreens or coniferous plants. You want different heights and widths in your shrubs so that the landscaping doesn't appear monotonous. You also want your landscaping to complement your home, not compete with it.

Make sure you have plenty of flowers. It's a good idea to stagger the flowers in size as well: taller flowers towards the back, medium height in the middle and short in the front. This multi-tiered effect brings out the beauty of all of the flowers at once and also naturally draws the eyes to your home. Different types of flowers also create texture, without even having to touch the flowers this variation of textures appeals to our buyer's sense of touch as well as sight.

In addition to visually drawing the eyes to the home, you want the landscaping to specifically draw eyes to the front door. There are different ways to do this, but one good way is to have plantings going up in height as they move towards the front door.

When you choose your flowers and shrubs, pick a few that have a pleasant fragrance. Don't choose anything too overpowering and not a collision of fragrances that will end up competing with each other. Just a nice, pleasant scent that will register on the buyer's senses as they walk toward your front door.

If it is winter and you have snow, then make sure your drive and walkways are shoveled and clear of snow (you won't need to mess with the flowers or shrubs!).

## Wendy's Wisdom

*It never ceases to amaze me how many older homes have NO landscaping! However, no landscaping is probably preferable to one that hasn't been taken care of. As my sister Julie says, "I like to put my own gardening stamp on my yard and I don't want to clean up someone else's mess."*

### Mulch, Mulch, Mulch

Let's cover this one more time, since it is so important and affordable to do. After you have pulled all of the weeds, trimmed all of the shrubs and trees and planted a ton of flowers you want to mulch the bejeepers out of it. Mulch is inexpensive and it can make even older landscaping look fresh. You don't want to see exposed soil anywhere. Cover it all with a nice layer of mulch.

The other thing mulch does for us is to create a natural border between our lawn (or rocks or whatever) and our plantings. This border creates a defined landscaping space without having to spend a boatload of cash on pavers and retaining walls. After all, we want our landscaping to look great to buyers without having to go broke doing it.

You want your home to stand out from your neighbors, but in a good way. Take a walk around your neighborhood and look at the landscaping of the nicest homes in your neighborhood. Ignore the tens of thousands of dollars spent on fancy pavers, decks and retaining walls, focus on the affordable things they did to make their landscaping look great. As a side note, when you take that walk around the neighborhood and check out your neighbor's landscaping you should probably just stick to looking at their front yards. They might not appreciate your snooping around their back yard.

*Don't let the neighbors catch you peeking!*

There are a couple of other ways to get great ideas for designing your landscaping. The first is your television. No I don't mean planting your TV in your front lawn, although sometimes given the quality of a lot of shows it would be worth it.

What I mean is watch a few TV shows about landscaping. The DIY Network and HGTV are two great stations where you can get tons of ideas. Another great option is to go to your local bookstore and look through home and garden magazines. You'll see some amazing landscaping photos. Use them to get ideas for AFFORDABLE things you can do to improve your landscaping. Look at how the shrubs and flowers are laid out. Are there particular plants that really catch your eye? If so they may well catch the buyer's eye as well.

Go to your computer and Google "Landscape Design Ideas". You will find over 694,000 entries. That should keep you busy.

**Front Yard Versus Back Yard**

While your front yard is all about curb appeal your back yard should be all about creating a haven; an oasis. It should be inviting. A place where your buyers want to spend time relaxing.

In Chapter 3, I suggested putting a small, bistro style table or even a full size patio table with some chairs in the yard or on the deck. You can take that a step further by setting that table with colorful place settings whenever you can before showings. Just don't leave these out between showings or they'll get all dirty and ruin the effect. Also put a small vase with some flowers and light a couple of candles (if the showing is in the evening) as center pieces on the table.

If you already have a table but it's kind of weather worn from sitting outside, put a table cloth on it. It's a lot cheaper than replacing the table and a table cloth that is well coordinated with the place settings will work very nicely.

*You don't need much to make the space look inviting!*

Other nice ideas are hanging a hammock or a comfortable swing in a nice shaded spot, adding some planters on the deck or around the table if you don't have a deck. If you have a children's play area in the yard make sure it isn't strewn with toys. Take the time to keep it cleaned up. Outdoor fire pits are popular right now; either the chimneas or the fire table styles. If you have one, set it out with some pieces of wood laid out as though it were ready to go. Then set a few chairs around it.

All of the rules about lawn care, weed elimination, and trimming shrubs apply to the backyard as well as the front.

**Some No No's**

A few things to put away while you are selling your home:

- Garden gnomes, pink flamingos, gargoyles, plastic deer and other lawn art. Most people don't like lawn art, so removing your favorite pieces will be a smart move.
- Empty beer bottles, soda cans or whatever else is left over from your last yard party.

- Political statements or moral statements. It's okay to have political and moral opinions but if you are broadcasting those opinions on your front lawn when you are trying to sell your home, you'll be alienating at least 50% of your potential buyers.

- An excessive number of chairs or lawn furniture. You don't want things to look too cluttered.

- Motor homes, boats, 4-wheelers, snowmobiles and other large toys. If they are in the driveway or in any way blocking the buyer's view of your home, they should be moved off-site to a storage facility or friend or family member's house. The same goes for too many cars. If your driveway and garage are full of cars and car projects you'll want to clear them out before showings. See if a friend will let you store the extra ones with them while trying to sell your home.

**The Annoying Neighbor**

Do you have one of those neighbors who never seems to get around to mowing their lawn? Never pulls a weed unless it completely blocks their path into the house? Or, if they aren't that bad, do you have a next door neighbor whose yard and house is an eye sore?

Bad neighbors can be murder when it comes to selling your home. You go to all of this hard work to make your house and yard look great so you can get your home sold and theirs looks like crud. You know that every time a buyer comes to look at your house they are staring at the neighbor's house and thinking, "I really don't want a neighbor like that."

What do you do? You can certainly ask your neighbor to take better care of their yard, but I wouldn't expect to have tremendous success with that. The best thing I can recommend is that you offer to mow their lawn and pull their weeds for them while you are trying to sell your home. Just explain to them that while you are trying to sell your home you want things to look really good and that you would be happy to take care of their lawn at the same time you take care of yours. You can also just mow it one day while they are at work and leave a note on their door saying, "Welcome home! Someone decided to make your day and give you a FREE lawn mowing. May your day tomorrow be just as fruitful." It will appear that someone did a nice deed for them versus asking to do it and potentially offending them. You decide based on your neighbors and what will work best with them.

Sometimes it's a real pain being nice to inconsiderate neighbors, but just remember if you can get your house sold by mowing their lawn, they won't be your neighbor anymore.

## Home Exterior

As important as the landscaping is, we can't ignore the face of our home either. The landscaping draws the eyes to the front of the home, the entrance. It's important that the entrance look appealing and well maintained.

This is a good time to clean up clutter around the front. If you have a garden hose, sprayer, or anything else laying around, put them away. Clean and tidy. The front entrance should have a nice, new, clean welcome mat. Sweep up the front porch or steps and keep it clean.

I recommend investing a little bit of money to get a new, MATCHING front porch light, mailbox, house numbers and maybe even a door knocker. They will create a very favorable impression on your potential tenant-buyers. If you can't replace them make sure you clean up the existing ones, no layers of paint caked on and so forth. I also recommend putting a few planters or hanging baskets on your front porch or front steps with inviting flowers. Every day or so, water and trim plants and flowers, and clean up the entire area.

I used the word "clean" about 6 times in the last two paragraphs, deliberately. Keeping things clean is one of the most important things you can do when it comes to selling your home. The best part is, it costs nothing to do it, but time.

## Wendy's Wisdom

*Buyers don't want to see messes. They don't want to buy someone else's dirt - so CLEAN!*

If you have a large enough front porch I recommend setting out a couple of chairs or a front porch swing. Think about adding some wind chimes to appeal to the buyer's sense of sound. If you have any old junk sitting on your front porch like broken down furniture, or worse, old appliances, car parts, a motorcycle in the process of being rebuilt, GET RID OF THEM. I don't care where you live, a broken down old refrigerator sitting on the front porch is not a selling point.

Aside from the front entrance we have the rest of the face of the house. I mentioned it in the last chapter – power wash your house. Make sure it's clean (yep, there's that "clean" word again). Any areas that have caulk on them, like seams around windows and door frames should receive a fresh coat of caulk if the old caulk is dirty, breaking up or missing entirely.

Every window on the house should be cleaned both inside and out. They should sparkle. If you have storm windows and the weather is warm, take them off and put on the screens. If it is cold out make sure you clean the storm windows too. All of the screens should be in good condition with no holes or tears and cleaned as well. Some people feel that you shouldn't have the screens on so that buyers can see out the sparkly windows better. I prefer to see the screens so I know they exist, but I'll let you make that choice.

Do you have shutters bordering your windows on the face of your house? If you don't have shutters you should really consider adding them, they can help make a plain house look more impressive. Most homes look better with shutters. If you already have shutters but they are dull or worn, consider giving them a fresh coat of paint. Make sure your existing shutters or new shutters are an appropriate color selection to coordinate with your trim, siding and front door.

## Wendy's Wisdom

*All home improvement stores have paint cards to show coordinating colors for the outside of your home. These will help you pick colors that will match with what you already have.*

## Inside

We've spent a lot of time outside, giving your home curb appeal, but really not very much money. I tried to pack in as many ideas as possible because you really do want your house to capture the buyer's interest from the outside so that you can get them inside. We had ideas that appealed to 4 of the 5 senses outside, sight, touch, smell and sound. Now let's appeal to the last sense, taste.

Frank McKinney is a real estate investor/builder who builds ultra-luxurious, multimillion dollar, ocean front mansions and sells them to the super wealthy. He builds them "on spec", meaning that the future homeowner isn't determined until the house is built and he tries to sell it. He is enormously successful in this luxurious home building business and selling them on spec.

The reason I bring him up now is that one of the things he does when showing his homes is to have a bowl of wrapped chocolates at the front entryway and encourages his prospective buyers to enjoy them, appealing to their sense of taste. While he does this in ultra-luxury homes there isn't any reason we can't do it in our more modest homes. After all, a bag of wrapped chocolates only costs a few dollars, but what a nice way for buyers to be greeted as they come in to view your home. Put them into a nice bowl and have them by the front door.

Turn a small radio to a jazz station and have it playing low in the kitchen. Appeal to every sense including the sense of sound (this is not the time to "rock" out with a heavy metal station!). Even if you don't live there you should leave it playing 24/7.

Before we go through your home room by room, let's go over some general rules of home staging that apply to every room of the house first.

## Clutter Me Not

One of the most important things to do when it comes to making the inside of your home look desirable is to get rid of the clutter. After living in our home for a while we tend to accumulate stuff. We have stacks of stuff, shelves of stuff, closets full of stuff, boxes full of stuff. Since you are going to be moving anyway this is the perfect time to go through your stuff and have a yard sale and make some donations. In other words, you need to start getting rid of some of your stuff!

I have heard professional home stagers recommend that the average home owner clear about 1/3 of their possessions out of the house before putting it on the market. Some of us are bigger pack rats than others so you may need to clear out more than that. Definitely remove any collections of dolls, spoons, Star Wars figures, or any other dust catchers. Rent one of those portable storage containers, PODS or the like, and move a bunch of your non-essential stuff into it. Once you've loaded it up they'll haul it away and store it for you until you move into your new home, where you'll be free to clutter again.

Clutter makes rooms look smaller. We want each room and every closet in our house to look as spacious as possible. Clutter also overwhelms a space and keeps a potential buyer from really being able to see the space over the clutter.

### Clean Me Up, Scotty

I mentioned cleaning with regards to the exterior of the house. It is doubly important inside. Clear the cobwebs, dust every nook and cranny, scrub away the mildew, vacuum, sweep and mop, and just make your whole house look clean. It costs absolutely nothing but it makes such a big difference. Remember, buyers don't want to buy someone else's dirt. Even if you are selling your home as a fixer-upper and intend to put no money into it at all, clear all the clutter and clean everything up. That will go a long way towards finding a better quality tenant-buyer and help you get a better price.

### Window Treatments

It's a good idea to have window treatments on every window in the house, if they make sense. The last two homes I have lived in I didn't have them on the back of my home. One was a lakefront home and one is wooded acreage. I didn't want to cover my view and no one can see in unless they are walking in my backyard, which would be very rare.

A combination of blinds with curtains is best. But here's the catch, you also want to let lots of light into the house too. So the blinds should be raised and the curtains fully open. This creates a nice framing effect on each window. Go with gauzy or light window treatments versus heavy draperies. Also, extend your curtain rods beyond the window borders so that most of the drapery is actually beyond the window, this makes the window look bigger and allows more light into the room.

### Lighting

In addition to letting in natural light you want to add plenty of artificial light. The trick that home stagers use is to layer the lighting. They use a blend of light from ceiling fixtures, lamps, wall lights and task lights. You want to make rooms bright, without being too bright and not have any single light source overly stand out. You can also use lighting to highlight an important feature of a room. For example, if you have a beautiful fireplace you can increase the light around it to brighten the fireplace in comparison to the rest of the room. This helps naturally draw buyer's eyes to your highlight.

*This room is an excellent example of layered lighting with a chandelier, bed-side lamps and recessed ceiling lights*

### Doorknobs, Switch Plates and Outlet Covers, Oh My!

If you painted your walls and doors like I suggested in the last chapter, did you paint over your old light switches and outlets? This is one of my pet peeves. If you are going to go to all of the trouble to make the walls and doors look great, you should finish the job by replacing all light switch plates and outlet covers with new ones. I also recommend replacing all of the doorknobs if they look at all worn, because it's so inexpensive to do it. The reason this is a pet peeve of mine is that freshly painted walls with painted over switches and outlets looks like a cover up job to me, however, freshly painted walls with brand new switch plates and outlet covers makes the walls look brand new. Doorknobs work the same way with doors.

Replacing all of the switch plates and outlet covers in your home should cost you about $30. If any of the actual light switches or outlets are beat up or painted over I recommend replacing those as well. It's pretty easy to do and not very expensive (maybe another $20 to $30 for the whole house).

## Wendy's Wisdom

*If you are going to replace the light switches and outlet plates, make sure you TURN OFF THE POWER FIRST! You will have a little surprise if you don't.*

### *Arranging the Furniture*

If you've ever seen a professional home stager in action they seem to have this great ability to take the existing furnishings you have and rearrange them, sometimes into different rooms and make your home look completely different--and so much better. Because the furnishings you have and the layout of the rooms in your home will be completely different for each person there aren't a lot of general tips I can give you for arranging your furniture.

I'll talk about using a professional home stager at the end of the chapter, but if you are going it alone I recommend trying several things. Look in home magazines. It doesn't cost anything to go to the bookstore and look at them. They are full of photos that can give you great ideas. The advertisement photos in the magazines can be some of the best because even though they are advertising a particular home product they are usually showing it in a fully staged room.

Another great option to get more tidbits is on TV. HGTV in particular has really come to realize that the housing market has gone soft and they have multiple shows now exclusively focusing on home staging. These stagers share tons of useful tips and tricks for making your home look great. What I don't recommend doing is going out and buying whole new furniture sets for key rooms in your home just for staging. This is not the best way to spend your money. A few small purchases here and there may really go a long way towards changing the feel of a room, but I would leave it at that.

There are a few commonsense tips I can offer that apply, no matter what furnishings you have and how the layout of a room is.

1. *Don't leave large dead spaces*. This is where you have things arranged such that a chunk of the room is cut off or useless. You want to maximize your room space and include all of it. If you make the space look non-functional your potential buyers will see it as non-functional, too.

2. *Clearing the clutter applies to too much furniture as well*. Too much furniture in a room makes it look small and uninviting. Also, multiple uses for a room counts as clutter too, mental clutter. Focus on a dedicated purpose for the room and keep the amount of furniture functional, but uncluttered.

3. *Don't have everything pushed up against the walls*. This actually goes against common sense, but it is one of the great tricks of home stagers. In common rooms arrange your furnishings away from the walls while creating traffic flow. It makes the room more visually appealing while also not creating a large dead space in the center of the room which happens when everything is pushed against walls. Contrary to what you may think it also makes the room look larger.

### Artwork

It's a good idea to have some tasteful but eye catching artwork on the walls around your entryway, but not too big. We don't want the art to overwhelm the room. You also want to arrange art on the walls in something of a non-conventional fashion. Most rooms have art all set at the same height and spaced somewhat evenly around a room. This practically renders the art invisible to your buyer's eyes. Mix it up a little bit. Arrange the art at different heights in groupings. Stagger them to create a visual eye-line towards a highlight of the room. Use the art in tandem with pieces of furniture to pull them all together. Get ideas from TV or magazines. As long as the centers of the artwork or groupings are eye-level, it will look good.

### *Entryway*

Now that we've gone over general ideas, let's look at specific rooms. We'll start off where the buyers first come into your home, the entryway. If your family also enters the house through the main entryway it's likely going to be cluttered with shoes, coats, purses, hats, junk mail, etc. This is just the kind of clutter I was talking about cleaning up. Take all of your non-seasonal items and pack them up – in other words, if you are selling your house during the summer, pack up all of the winter jackets, hats, boots, scarves and so forth. You want to keep a small amount of things in the closet so it looks used but not too much that it looks even remotely cluttered.

As a side note, if you pack up a whole bunch of jackets, don't leave the empty hangers in the closet. If your family's main entry is someplace else in the house like a side or back door, you'll want to clear this clutter out from there.

Remember the bowl of chocolates? Along with those cut some fresh flowers and put them in a vase behind the chocolates. Right next to these, you can put some flyers outlining the features of the house as well as terms for the rent-to-own purchase. In addition to letting in natural light from the front entry, you'll also want a nice ceiling fixture and possibly a small accent lamp as well. How much light your entry needs will depend on its size, so you'll need to make that decision.

## *Living Rooms, Family Rooms and Dens*

These common spaces should focus on making the buyer feel comfortable. Make it inviting; a space to relax. If these spaces are small in your home, use a few key pieces of furniture to make the space seem cozy, but definitely minimize the clutter. If you have a large space, you may want to arrange the furniture so it is divided into multiple sections; possibly an area for home theater and also a reading nook or something like that. Remember to make use of artwork and lighting to help contribute to the sense of space. Think about layering textures by adding decorative pillows or throw blankets on your furniture. If you choose different materials with different textures that compliment each other, you can appeal to your buyer's sense of touch.

## *Master Bedroom*

The master bedroom is the ultimate refuge. It is the haven within the home. No matter how large or small your master bedroom is, you want it to appeal to the buyers as a place they WANT to spend their nights. A common problem many small master bedrooms have is to be overwhelmed with furniture and clutter. In addition to the bed, there are night stands, multiple dressers and the closet is crammed full. This does not make for an oasis.

If your master bedroom is cramped, it's time to move some of the furniture out. Obviously you have to have a bed in there, but if you have a king-sized bed in a pint-sized bedroom, you may want to swap out for a queen-sized bed, if you have one in another room. If you've got more than one dresser you may want to move the extras out.

Also, closets are a big selling point for houses. Buyers want to know that they have plenty of closet space for their stuff. If your master bedroom closet is jam–packed, buyers will look at it and decide there just isn't enough room for their stuff, even if your closets are huge. Clear your closets out. Take out all of the off season clothes. Highlight the closet's functionality. Have just enough things on the shelves and things hanging up to make it seem

73

like the closet could hold so much more, but don't have so little that it's barren. Take boxes of extra stuff to family and friends to store. If your home is vacant, rent, borrow, or use your things to stage the rooms and closets for visual appeal.

## Bathrooms

Your bathrooms should be so clean you can eat off the floor (but no need to test it this way!). There shouldn't be any mildew, soap scum, toilet rings, body hair or anything else that makes the buyers think they are buying your dirt. Make sure the mirrors sparkle.

If your bathroom has a window - that's great. Let in lots of natural light. Many bathrooms suffer from only having one garishly bright light fixture. This is the perfect room to bring in additional sources of light to create layers. You may even want to put lower watt bulbs in the one fixture that is overly bright once you have other light sources in the room.

I don't know about you, but my bathroom counter has about a million things on it: toothpaste, toothbrushes, razors, and lotions, soap, Kleenex, contact lens solution, more lotions, hair brushes, makeup, deodorant, and more lotions -- in other words clutter. The cabinets are even worse. Look at the pictures of bathrooms in home magazines. Do they look at all like your bathroom? Not mine. They look like what I wish my bathroom could look like. The counters have about three things on them and they are all decorative. There is beautiful artwork on the walls. And nice, plush towels are set out.

Yes, they have really expensive sinks and vanities and super fancy showers and all that, but that's not what we are looking for. Look at what you can do with your existing bathroom without having to dump a ton of money into new fixtures. Focus on how they are decorated. It's time to take out your good towels. You know, the ones that only come out when you have guests. Clear out all of your stuff. Clear the counters off and only have a few decorative accents. I know this is going to be painful, but you need to clear a lot of stuff out of the cabinets, too. Buyers are going to look there, so the clutter needs to be packed away. Like the closets, you don't have to eliminate everything, but you need to clear out enough so that the storage space looks functional without being overcrowded. A good way to do this is to clear out some of each type of thing, clear out some of the towels without packing away all of them; some of the lotions and creams, etc.

### *Kitchen*

"Kitchens and baths sell homes." Pretty much any real estate agent in the country will agree with this. Making your kitchen look the absolute best it can is well worth it when you are trying to sell your home. The beautiful thing about staging your kitchen is that you really don't have to spend any money to do it. In the last chapter we talked about making improvements to your kitchen, but here we are just going to focus on the finishing touches – turning your kitchen into something that your rent-to-own buyers really love.

I'm going to send you back to the bookstore to look at home magazines again. Those pictures will give you a ton of great ideas. Also, check www.hgtv.com. They have a section called "Rate My Space" where other homeowners post photos of their homes. There are thousands of kitchen photos. My recommendation is to sort them by the top rated pictures. There you will see what other homeowners did to make their kitchens look gorgeous.

Most of the time our counters are loaded with stuff we use all of the time in the kitchen, as well as junk mail, school papers, and all kinds of other things from everyday life. It's all got to go. We want to maximize our counter space, especially in small kitchens with limited counters. By clearing everything possible off the counters we make them look much more usable. If you look at photos of well-staged kitchens about the only things you see on the counters are a few decorative accents. The kitchen should get the best of your home's decorations - bring them in from other rooms of the house if necessary.

You also want to empty all of the infrequently used things out of the cabinets. Pack them away in anticipation of your upcoming move. Buyers like to see plenty of cabinet space and you can help give them that impression by eliminating a lot of the stuff inside your cabinets.

Cleaning is also essential. Keep your kitchen spotless. If you have a stainless steel sink, get some stainless steel polish (only costs a couple of dollars) to make your kitchen sink look brand new.

You'll also want to clean INSIDE as well as the outside of your appliances and inside the cabinets, maybe even put down a new layer of shelf paper.

If you have wood-finished cabinets, there is an inexpensive product called Cabinet Magic® (you can find this in the cleaning products isle of most home improvement stores) that can really help to clean up and freshen the finish on the face of your cabinets. You also want to make the best possible use of layering of lights in the kitchen. Your kitchen should be warm and bright. For just a little money, you can get some under-the-cabinet lights that really help bring light to the countertops, and highlight your decorative accents. You can buy plug-in "hockey puck" style under-cabinet lights that you can install yourself. They cost $20 to $40.

The kitchen is a great space to appeal to the sense of smell. I've heard that the most popular smells that really resonate with buyers are that of apple pie or pumpkin pie. I'm not suggesting that you bake an apple pie every time you have a showing, (although if you hold an open house, it might not be a bad idea). You can always buy a frozen one instead of making it from scratch. What I do recommend is something like an apple spice or pumpkin spice scented candle.

**A Few Obvious Things**

We've gone through the entire house now to look at many things you can do to stage your home. Most cost nothing to do. We need to look at a few obvious things when it comes to preparing your home for sale that you need to make sure you do. I say they are obvious, but there are always some sellers who overlook them, so I feel they are worth mentioning. All of these suggestions come from things either I've encountered or heard of other real estate agents encountering during showings.

- *Scoop the poop* - anytime you have a showing you should always make sure there isn't any dog poop in your yard. What buyer is going to want to buy your home after they step in dog doo? Even worse, what if they track it in your house! Empty the cat litter boxes, too – they stink! Pet owners are notorious for not noticing their own cat and dog smells, but the rest of the world notices when they walk into their homes. Think about this. It can cost you thousands of dollars to have a pet odor in your home, maybe even the loss of any sale. Deodorize and clean up their messes.

- *Hide the bongs* - your lifestyle preferences are your own, however, you shouldn't leave any drug paraphernalia out where potential buyers can see it.

- *Dogs Playing Poker is NOT high art* - when I talk about putting artwork on your walls, this does not include a velvet Elvis or a print of Dogs Playing Poker. Repairs - Three Strikes and You're Out!

- Put away the personal/intimate toys or anything else x-rated. Do you really want potential buyers and real estate agents knowing what you are up to?

- *Don't forget what time your showings are* - I've heard of an agent and prospective buyers walking in on an amorous couple who forgot what time the showing was scheduled for! Don't be home during showings.

  Obviously, if you are selling your home yourself you need to be there. But if you have your home listed with an agent, don't be there when the buyers come to look around. Buyers don't like it when sellers are looking over their shoulders.

# Hiring a Professional Home Stager

This is a business that has been growing by leaps and bounds in recent years. Professional home stagers are not yet available in all areas, but if you can find one in your area you may want to consider hiring a pro. In many cases, home stagers can make use of your existing furnishings and yet make your home look better than you ever imagined. Some home stagers also have an inventory of furnishings that they can bring into your home. They can sell or rent you items for your home. Pricing can vary greatly as can quality of the stager.

Home stagers aren't particularly regulated at this point nor are they all trained from one location, some may have no training at all. Visit www.IAHSP.com to find members in your area.[ii] If you are going to make use of a pro, I suggest you ask for references and also look at some of their work to decide if they are right for you. Ask your real estate agent for a recommendation, if they haven't already provided you with one.

## How to Stage Your Home If You've Already Moved Out

If you have already moved out and your home is vacant, there are still some tricks you can use to help increase the appeal of your home. Obviously, moving all of the furniture back into the house isn't really a workable option - after all you need it. However, if you do have a few pieces to spare that you can use to properly stage one or two rooms it may be worth it. If you don't have any, then borrow from a friend or relative.

The best thing to do with a vacant home is to make use of the decorative accents. You can still put art on the walls and decorative touches on countertops. Add live or artificial plants in the right places. Only use live plants if you are close enough to water them regularly. You still want to make the best use of layered lighting you possibly can.

In other words, just because your home is empty doesn't mean you can't decorate it. Any real estate agent will tell you that empty homes just do not show as well as occupied or staged homes. Even if you don't rent-to-own your home, this chapter should help you sell it for more and quicker. It is all about standing out in the buyer's mind.

Another possibility, if it's in your budget, is to hire a professional home stager that has their own inventory to furnish and stage your home. This can be costly, so you'll want to evaluate whether you think it's a worthwhile step toward getting your home sold.

We have covered a lot of ground in the last few chapters. Following some of these guidelines will help you sell your home, whether rent-to-own or a traditional sale. It's all about standing out in the buyer's mind.

I know this chapter was jammed packed with information. Remember, you don't need to do everything. Focus on key elements that stand out the most in your home (and with your budget) to really catch the attention of your rent-to-own buyers. Now that we have your home properly staged we can move on to setting a price. This can be exciting when selling your home as a rent-to-own because you may be able to get more money for your home!

# Chapter 5

## Pricing and Rental Rates

If you are listing your home for sale, how do you determine what your asking price should be? There are many answers to this question. Unfortunately very few of them are right. What's worse if you go with the wrong answer you'll either under-price your home costing you thousands to tens of thousands of dollars or you'll over-price your home and it will never sell which will cost you thousands, possibly tens of thousands.

### Wendy's Wisdom

*While pricing your home may seem like a scary prospect, it shouldn't be. Use a real estate agent to guide you through this process.*

### How Do You Determine a Home's Value?

*Taxable Basis*

In most states there are values determined by the tax assessor's office. It might be called your tax value, assessed value or something similar. That number might not be 100% of the property value. Usually there is some type of formula that each city or state uses.

Some homeowners that try the "For Sale by Owner" route use the taxable basis when determining the asking price of their home. This technique is a little bit more accurate than a blind person doing target practice with a bazooka, in other words, if you are pointed in the right direction you'll be close enough to do some damage.

Unfortunately using the taxable basis fails to take into account a number of things, like:

1. What are homes actually worth in your neighborhood

2. The condition of your home

3. What upgrades have been made to your home

4. What the real estate market in your neighborhood is actually doing

As you might be able to guess, all of these factors can have a huge impact on the value of your home and would be in no way reflected on the taxable basis. The result, your home will either be over or under priced.

### Zillow, Trulia, Yahoo, Eppraisal and a Slew of Others

There are a lot of real estate websites out there now that claim they can give you a value for your home. Some of them are more harmless than others. What I mean by that is that some of the sites will only give you a possible value range while others will try to give you an actual number. The sites that give you a value range are relatively harmless if the range is broad enough because you won't be able to really choose the price based on that range. The ones that give you an actual number - I won't name names, but if you go to these sites and enter your address you'll see which ones I'm talking about – will cause you the most harm. This is because that number is quite likely to be *entirely wrong!*

Just for the fun of it go to these websites and try to get your home's value from them. I did it on my home with 4 different sites and got 4 different values, with a range of over $80,000! I certainly don't want to under price or over price my home by $80,000.

## *Your Neighbors*

Another method I have seen employed quite often is to price a home's value based on what your nearby neighbors are trying to sell their homes for, and then almost always adding some. Why would you add some? Of course, your home is better, right? It might be and it might not be. But most sellers think their home is nicer or more updated than their neighbors. Be careful with this, as it can be a dangerous way to price your home.

Unfortunately, this method makes several assumptions that will likely lead to pricing trouble:

1. You arc assuming that your neighbors' homes are priced accurately

2. You are assuming that your home is genuinely comparable to your neighbors

3. You are assuming that whatever pricing differential you make between you and your neighbors is an accurate reflection of the differences in the homes covering lot size, home size, home condition, improvements, etc.

Even if you happen to live in a neighborhood of identically sized ranch houses with identical lots, there can still be pricing differences based on the condition and improvements in the home. If you have a finished basement or a newly remodeled kitchen, you need to be able to accurately set a value for those improvements.

## *Appraisal*

An appraisal is probably the most accurate way of determining a home's value. While it seems to be the most costly in the short term, what it can save you in the long run by having your home accurately priced offsets the upfront cost.

If you are going to sell your home on a "For Sale by Owner" basis, I cannot encourage you enough to have an appraisal done.

When you get it done, make sure you ask for a market value appraisal. This will give you the closest possible pricing guide for your home.

Just be aware that while appraisals are far more accurate than trying to guestimate your home's value on your own, they can vary as well. I sold one home a few years ago (not on a rent-to-own basis) that, when I had it appraised, the value came in at $155,000. I set my asking price at $159,900 and sold it for $155,000 a few months later. When the buyer's lender had it appraised, their appraiser set the value at $179,000! That's a difference of $24,000. Does that mean that I under priced my home?

I don't think so. The appraiser I used actually lived in that neighborhood and knew it quite well, while the bank's appraiser was from a nearby city.

## *Real Estate Agents*

 Making use of a real estate agent can be an excellent way to determine the value of your home. Real estate agents, like appraisers, actually look at recent comparables and look at your home to determine how its condition affects its value and then suggest a price before listing your home. They will perform an analysis of value, for no charge in most cases.

Sounds simple enough, but unfortunately there is a bit more to it. If a real estate agent is competing with other real estate agents to get you to agree to list your home with them, some agents may suggest listing it for a higher price as an inducement to get the listing. Does this mean that your home will sell for more by listing it for more? Of course not.

What it means is that your home is going to sit on the market for a long time until the agent gets you to agree to reduce the asking price. Real estate agents refer to this as "chasing the market." This can cost you more if your market is down.

When you chase a market, you end up chasing the down turn and it will cost you more than pricing it "ahead of the market" from day one. In other words, if you want to sell your home, don't ask for top dollar in a down market. You should price it a little *lower* than what it is worth today. Otherwise your market pricing will drop below where it is now, and you will be "chasing the market" when you decide to reduce your price.

When you meet with an agent, ask to see "comparables". They should show you recent sales comparables as well as what is currently on the market. Ask the agent WHY they are suggesting a particular price. Also ask them what you should expect to receive for a sales price on your home. A good real estate agent should easily be able to justify the asking price with accurate comparables and condition analysis of your home.

In some cases your real estate agent may recommend that you order an appraisal to determine the best price. They may do this if the comparables aren't very strong, if your home is significantly different, or if your market is changing rapidly.

Sometimes real estate agents are subject to pricing pressures from the home seller. Some sellers have a price fixed in their mind that they either need or want and insist that the home be listed for that price. Some agents will still take the listing, hoping to get the home seller to agree to reduce the price down the road.

This doesn't work.

If you are trying to sell your home you will have to face the reality of your home's market value. If you try to force your real estate agent to list the home for the price you want, it will sit on the market for a long time and may never sell. And, even if you happen to find a buyer that is willing to pay your price (good luck!), you still won't actually get that price, and here's why: When the buyer tries to get a mortgage on your home his lender will order an appraisal. The appraisal will reflect the actual market value of your home, NOT the agreed upon sales price between you and the buyer. In the "Boom Years" there was fudge room in appraisals, but not anymore. If your home doesn't appraise for enough the lender will not give the buyer a mortgage. That means either you will need to reduce the selling price of your home to the appraised value or the sale will fall apart.

## Wendy's Wisdom

*The best methods for setting the price or your home are either an appraisal or a real estate agent's comparables. While they may cost money, they will certainly save you in the long run.*

Unfortunately, none of these methods of determining your home's value are 100% fool proof. While appraisals and comparables are the most accurate, even those can't reflect every single variation. The true value of your home is set by what you, as the seller, agree to sell it for and what the buyer agrees to buy it for (as long as the lender's appraisal agrees). Our effort in setting the asking price of our rent-to-own home is designed to get the best possible price with the shortest time on the market.

### Rent-to-Own Premium

There is an important factor to remember when setting the asking price of your home, the rent-to-own premium. Because you are offering your home for sale on a rent-to-own basis, you will most likely be able to ask for a slightly higher price than market value.

How much more you can ask will depend on the conditions of the market you are selling in:

- ***Hot Market*** - Heavily favors sellers. You may be able to get an additional 5% to 10% above the current value (not including any appreciation)

- ***Flat Market*** - Favors neither buyers nor sellers. You can probably expect an additional 3% to 5% above the current value

- ***Down Market*** - Market heavily favors buyers. You would likely get 0% to 5% price premium above the current value.

### *Another Factor to Consider in Your Pricing*:

### How Much do You Owe?

If you owe close to what you can sell your home for, or more than what you can sell your home for, you will need to take this into account. Selling your home on a rent-to-own basis may be the best option for you in this case. Not only do you get to add in the rent-to-own price premium, but it also gives you time to make additional payments on the house to help pay down the principal balance of the mortgage.

Even taking the price premium and principal pay down into account you will need to plan for the final balance of your mortgage at the end of the option period compared to the selling price of the home. If you will still owe more on your mortgage than you can sell the house for you will have to be able to cover the difference.

### *Rental Rates*

In addition to setting your asking price you also need to determine how much to ask each month for rent. Setting accurate rental rates can be just as challenging as setting the asking price for your home. If you are trying to do it on your own, you'll find that it's harder to find comparables.

## Wendy's Wisdom

*This is another reason I recommend using a real estate agent when selling your rent-to-own home. Not only can they save you money with accurate pricing, but they also can save you a lot of headaches and stress that come with having to try to figure many things out on your own. You will have a guide that can be worth his or her weight in gold.*

I've found that most people set their monthly rent based on what their monthly payment on the home is. Unfortunately that has little to no bearing on what the rent should be.

If your neighborhood has a lot of rental homes, you'll be able to get a fairly clear idea of what rental ranges are. If your area has few rental homes it will be much more difficult to do on your own.

If you order an appraisal on your home, it is also possible to get the appraiser to provide market rental rates for the home as part of the appraisal for an additional cost.

A real estate agent (one that is a property manager) is probably going to be one of your best bets when it comes to setting the monthly rent. She will have access to other homes for rent in the MLS and ones that are not on the MLS, and to help you determine a fair market rent for your rent-to-own home.

The internet is an excellent source for finding *rental comps* (comparable rental properties) if you are going the "For Sale by Owner" route. It is now one of the best places to advertise homes for

rent and for sale. The way to find out which sites are the best for your area – do a Google search and see what comes up. For instance: Rental Homes in San Diego. Look at the first 5-10 that come up.

You will also want to make use of these sites later when you are ready to advertise your home for sale, but for now what we are looking for are rental comps. See what is out there today. How do they compare to your home in terms of location, number of bedrooms and baths, and size. Then do a test ad. If a site is free (i.e. www.Craigslist.org) place an ad on your home. Try different rates. If you want $1,200.00 per month, test it. It won't be $1,200 if you live in San Diego, but you get the idea. If you get zero calls or very few, you might be too high or your ad is not worded very well (which I will cover in another chapter). If you get a ton of calls, your rental rate might be too low. Try another, slightly higher amount. I know this is not a very scientific way to determine the rate, but it does work, especially when there are not a lot of rental homes in your area.

### Rent-to-Own Premium

In some cases you will also be able to get a *rental premium* for your rent-to-own home. In other words, you'll be able to charge a little bit more in monthly rent than if the home were just a rental home. This is particularly the case in strong seller's markets or in an area with a shortage of rental homes.

## *Another Factor to Consider in Your Rental Rates*

While I said that setting your rent based on your monthly payment is not a good way to determine the rental rate, you do need to take into consideration what your monthly payment is. If your monthly mortgage payment, including taxes and insurance is too high, the monthly rent on your rent-to-own home may not be high enough to cover your entire payment. If this is the case you will need to cover that difference on your own. The *option fee* that the buyer pays up front can help cover this difference if the amount is not too great. I will cover the option fee in a later chapter.

So far I keep talking about using a Realtor® when selling your home as a rent-to-own, and you've seen some of the benefits. In the next chapter I focus specifically on using a real estate agent. I talk about the pros and cons as well as how to get your agent on board with rent-to-own, if you are already working with one.

# Chapter 6

## Using a Realtor®

Let's first start with how to pronounce this word. It is not "real-a-tor," it is "real-tor". There are two syllables in Realtor®, but most people pronounce it with three. All Realtors® are real estate agents, but not all real estate agents are Realtors®. In order to be a Realtor® you need to belong to the National Association of Realtors® (NAR). Realtors® take mandatory training every year and are required to adhere to a code of ethics. I use Realtor® and real estate agent interchangeably in this book, but it is important to understand that there can be a difference. If you are a real estate agent there is a section at the end of this book just for you.

If you do not have your home on the market yet, or are not currently using a real estate agent, you will need to evaluate whether you want to enlist an agent's help to sell your home on a rent-to-own basis. I think you will find that it will really help you with the sale of your home. Some of you might live far away from your home. In this case it is essential that you enlist the assistance of a real estate agent. If you are living in the home or living close by, you will probably still find the benefits far outweigh the expense.

If you are currently using a real estate agent to sell your home but haven't broached the rent-to-own subject with your agent yet, you can skip down to the "Getting Your Realtor® on Board" section. I also suggest giving them a copy of this book.

There are pros and cons to using a real estate agent. In my opinion, however, the pros definitely outweigh the cons. However, I will go over both sides so you can make the decision for yourself.

## Pros for Working with a Realtor®

### *Multiple Listing Service (MLS)*

The Multiple Listing Service (MLS) is a key benefit that real estate agents can offer their sellers. In addition to using it to provide comparables to help determine asking price and rental price, it is also the single greatest real estate marketing tool in existence. Most MLS systems feed into www.Realtor.com, which is one of the primary internet locations for searching for real estate.

Real estate agents use the MLS to list homes for sale and for rent. While rent-to-own homes are in the minority for listings, they are definitely growing in popularity, particularly in down markets. Additionally, if a buyer's agent is looking for a rent-to-own home for his clients, the MLS is where he goes to find them. If you want access to the large pool of buyers that real estate agents have, you need to have your home listed in the MLS.

### *Assistance with Paperwork*

*There isn't this much paperwork associated with selling your home, but if you try to do it all yourself it might seem that way.*

There is a lot of paperwork associated with selling your home, whether it is as a rent-to-own or a traditional sale. There is more paperwork with a rent-to-own. Each state and even some municipalities have specific requirements for what paperwork and contracts must be part of a real estate transaction. Real estate agents will know which clauses you should add to my contracts for your area.

In later chapters I will go into detail about essential rent-to-own contracts that need to be included in your transaction and where to get these forms. However, you will still need to make sure that you complete all of the paperwork necessary for selling your home.

## Wendy's Wisdom

*Use a real estate agent to handle the paperwork. If you are going the "For Sale by Owner" route, you should make use of an attorney to assist you. I don't recommend handling the paperwork on your own.*

In addition to making sure you have completed all of the necessary paperwork, a real estate agent can help you to make sure that the paperwork you complete gives you the protection you need. A common mistake people make is thinking all contracts are created equal. This is most often NOT TRUE. Making sure you have all of the proper terms and conditions in your contracts is absolutely critical.

For example, would you think it was possible for a buyer to make you pay for their annual trip to the Moose Droppings Festival in Talkeetna, Alaska? If the buyer wrote into their offer contract that you had to furnish them with round trip airline tickets and hotel reservations and you signed the contract without noticing it, would indeed be possible.

This is not meant to scare you. After all, I don't think there are too many buyers that even KNOW about the Moose Droppings Festival, let alone want to go.

Seriously, though, the average buyer knows very little about contracts and will almost always rely on whatever contracts their agent or the seller provides. You will want to provide the contracts for the deal, this way they are set up in your favor. I call these "pro-seller" contracts, which you can obtain on my website at www.wendypatton.com.

The point I'm trying to make is that just about any clause that appears in a real estate contract can be enforceable, so it is important that you have help with your contracts. I would strongly suggest that if you don't use a real estate agent you hire a real estate attorney for help with my contracts. If you want to save a ton on real estate attorney fees use my forms and have a "Pre-Paid Legal" attorney review them at *no charge*. Go to www.Prepaidlegal.com/hub/wendypatton for more information. These legal plans start at just $16.00 a month on a month-to-month basis, with no annual contract required.

## Wendy's Wisdom

*Not all contracts are created equal! Make sure you use the right contracts to protect yourself in the sale of your home. Even if your real estate agent wants to use their state approved contract (and they will) they can use the pro-seller clauses in my contracts to enhance theirs to favor you.*

### Comparables (Comps)

We talked about comps in the last chapter and how important they are when determining the asking price of your rent-to-own home. A real estate agent is one of your best resources for getting accurate comps.

### Staying Legal

Fair Housing Law is something that you as a home seller need to be in compliance with. The penalties for failing to do so can be quite severe. In chapter 15, I will go into some detail on Fair Housing Law to help you. The basics are that you must not discriminate against anyone based on their race, national origin, religion, sex, familial status, and/or disability. Additionally, many areas prohibit discrimination based on marital status, age and sexual orientation.

I think the penalties start with forcing you to go to the Moose Droppings Festival in Talkeetna. Just kidding, actually they are much worse. So make sure you stay legal.

Real estate agents are trained in Fair Housing Law and can really help you stay in compliance without having to worry about doing so on your own. Many people might not know that certain advertisements, questions on the phone to a prospect, or denying someone due to one of the above areas would be breaking the law.

### Let the Agent Do Your Showings

Until you have had to do a bunch of showings yourself, you'll never understand how much of a pain in the rump this can be, particularly when it's your own home you are trying to sell. It's a lot of frustration, time and effort, hoping to get that one showing that results in a sale.

### Negotiation Assistance

Real estate agents are experienced negotiators. A good agent that is representing you will help you with negotiations to get the best possible price and terms. A good real estate agent's expertise in negotiating can cover the cost of the commission alone. If you need a good real estate agent familiar with rent-to-own, go to my website, www.WendyPatton.com, follow the link to the rent-to-own site, and click on *Find a Real Estate Agent* or you can email my office at refer@wendypatton.com and we'll refer one to you.

### Cons of Working with a Realtor®

*Commission*

Of course, the biggest disadvantage to working with a real estate agent is having to pay them for their work, right?

## Wendy's Wisdom

*Real estate agents aren't greedy. Like the rest of us, they just want to get paid for their work.*

A good agent can earn their commission and more in the benefits to you. However, the cost of real estate commissions can be substantial. If the equity in your home is tight or if you owe more than you can sell your home for, this makes it very difficult to be able to afford the services of a real estate agent. Talk to your agent about your situation. Maybe they will help you for what you can afford (times are tough for them, too). Remember, rent-to-own homes often receive higher prices than regular sales and may help make the difference in being able to afford an agent.

If you are in the position of not being able to afford an agent, fear not. While I do recommend using a real estate agent when possible, you can still sell your rent-to-own home without one. You will just have to do all of the steps.

## Wendy's Wisdom

*Remember that if you are using a real estate agent and your tenant-buyer doesn't purchase the home, you don't have to pay the agent a commission (except the initial amount when the tenant-buyer moved in).*

### *Fighting an Uphill Battle*

If your agent doesn't understand how rent-to-own works or is resistant to helping you sell your home on a rent-to-own basis, you may be fighting an uphill battle to get them to agree to sell your home that way. Selling your home is difficult enough. Having to fight with your agent to do it makes it even more difficult. Just get another real estate agent! Remember, you can find a good one by emailing me at refer@wendypatton.com.

### *Time Lost*

Not all agents are created equal. Some of the biggest name real estate agents in your area may not be the best choice for listing your rent-to-own home. It is important to use an agent who will give you and your home the time and effort you deserve to find a rent-to-own buyer.

If you happen to select a poor quality agent, you may spend a lot of time with your home on the market and not get anywhere. Every month that your home sits is another mortgage payment, more utility payments, and so on. Even worse, if that agent fails to get the job done entirely, you may need to switch to another agent and start the process all over again. Ask the agent before you sign anything, what she can offer you to sell your home if it doesn't sell quickly or in the traditional way (meaning someone has cash or can get a mortgage).

By the way, if you do use a real estate agent for your rent-to-own sale and you are happy with her work, email my office at refer@wendypatton.com with their contact information and I will add them to my recommended real estate agent list.

### *Poor Priorities*

There are some agents out there who are much less interested in the quality of service they give you than in getting their commission.

These are the types of agents that never get referrals from satisfied customers, because most of their customers aren't satisfied.

When an agent places her commission first, she may push you into poor decisions. She may negotiate weakly to take no chances at losing a buyer; may recommend too low of a selling price, and so forth. Fortunately, most real estate agents aren't like that.

### Getting Your Realtor® on Board

Once you have made the decision to work with an agent you will need to get her to cooperate with you in selling your home as a rent-to-own. Not all agents understand how rent-to-own works. If your agent doesn't understand you'll need to help them understand the process. Buy them a copy of this book as a gift. It will help them sell your home. It will change the way they look at real estate forever.

Don't try to teach them yourself - make sure they read this book! Tell them they can't work with you until they do. Seriously, it will make your home selling experience much easier if they understand all aspects of this process. There are still many real estate agents that unfamiliar with this technique.

You will find that if you are trying to sell your home in a buyer's market it is much easier to get your real estate agent on board than in a seller's market. This is because homes are much harder to sell in a buyer's market and therefore real estate agents need to be more flexible and creative to get them sold.

### How They'll Get Paid

The first thing you need to do is to let your real estate agent know how they will get paid. Real estate agents as a group are not greedy, but they do want to be compensated for their work. The biggest hang up real estate agents have about doing rent-to-own sales is they don't understand how they will get paid.

Remember, since you are contracting the real estate agent to list your home, you call the shots, but you want your agent's support otherwise you'll be wasting your time with them. The best way to get their support is to reassure them about how they'll get paid. Typically you would pay the agent part of their commission at the onset of the option period and the remainder if the buyer purchases your home. Sometimes it's only the first month's rent. The most I would suggest you pay at the beginning of the option is 2% of the sales price (typically ½ of this goes to you agent's brokerage and the other ½ to the buyer's agent's brokerage), but the amount is negotiable with your agent. This amount usually would be paid out of the option fee you receive from the tenant-buyer. In this case you might not get much of the option fee up front. They can help you structure all of this after they read the part for real estate agents.

## Wendy's Wisdom

*You want to make sure that the commission paid at the onset comes off of their entire commission when it closes. Get this in writing in the listing contract. For instance, if the total commission is 6%, and you pay 2% upfront, then when the rent-to-own buyer closes, you will owe 4%.*

It is in the agent's best interest to help you negotiate a high option fee. The more the tenant-buyer puts down the more likely they will close (because if they don't the option fee is forfeited). You might even consider structuring the amount of commission paid upfront based on the amount of option fee you receive. That will give the agent a definite incentive to get you the best possible option fee. If you haven't signed up a real estate agent yet and the agent you are meeting with balks too much at the idea of rent-to-own, move on. There are other agents out there who will give you better service, without you having to fight them for it.

If you have already signed up with an agent and are trying to convince them to list your home on a rent-to-own basis, in addition to a regular sale, but are having trouble there are several things you can do:

1. Remind them that some commission in the short term and the rest later is much better than NONE at all if you can't get your home sold.
2. Suggest that your alternative is to just rent your home in which case they would get paid little to no commission at all.
3. Suggest you might cancel your agreement and find someone else. However, in any case, it's best to do this politely and diplomatically, instead of threatening.

An important point to be clear on is that you don't actually pay the agent directly. By law, a real estate agent is paid by the brokerage they work for. In fact, the listing contract for your home is with the agent's brokerage, not the agent. So in reality, you are paying the brokerage the commission and they pay their agent their portion. This is important because you would never write a check made out directly to that agent. You would write it to their office, for example: Keller Williams Realty Greater Chicago.

### *Prime* Your Realtor®

Once you have your agent on board, you both need to be speaking the same language. In other words, your agent will need to know about and understand the additional paperwork, points to negotiate and other steps necessary to selling your home on a rent-to-own basis. They will be on the same page with you after they read this book.

Now that we've gone through preparing your home, pricing your home and making the decision whether or not to use a real estate agent it's time to put it on the market. In the next chapter we'll focus on how to get the word out and start getting prospective rent-to-own buyers in your home.

# Chapter 7

## Marketing – Signs & Flyers, Newspaper, Internet, and Word of Mouth

When it comes to marketing your home you want to get the word out and you want maximum exposure so that you can get quick results. This means you'll want to explore multiple marketing options instead of just selecting one. The more potential buyers you reach the quicker you'll find your tenant-buyer and get an offer on your home.

### Go Beyond Your Real Estate Agent

Most people that list their home with a real estate agent leave it entirely up to their agent to market and sell their home. In hot markets this usually works for most sellers. In down markets this means that your time on market might be substantially longer and in the end you'll probably end up knocking your price down a few times before you get an offer. Who wants their home to sit on the market for eternity? It's not that your agent isn't doing their job; it's just that you have many other homes to compete with. Even when you make your home available on a rent-to-own basis with your agent, your exposure, while better, is still limited. Not all real estate agents will do everything to market your home. This chapter is something you can discuss with them and figure out a plan together.

### Maximize Exposure to get it Sold Fast

The real key to selling your rent-to-own home quickly is maximum exposure. The different marketing methods I'm going to talk about are almost all inexpensive or FREE. For the ones that cost money you'll need to decide how much you can afford; but for all of the others, since they are free, you should make every effort to do all of them. When advertising I use the *For Rent* and *For Sale* section of www.Craigslist.org and the newspaper. Try them both out to see what works best for you.

It's also a good idea to enlist the help of your real estate agent in these extra marketing efforts, you'll get even more exposure that way.

## Wendy's Wisdom

*I can't emphasize enough that you should take advantage of every type of free marketing you can. This is how to get your home sold FAST!*

### Newspaper – Old Reliable

The newspaper classified ads are probably the most expensive form of marketing your home, but they also work for many sellers. Most newspapers in addition to listing your ad in print also have a website which will show your ad.

People have long considered newspapers as one of the biggest sources for housing. So it's a good idea to have your home listed in this resource. There are ways to keep your cost down when it comes to newspaper ads. The first is to talk with the representative at the classified ads department to learn what types of ads work best and what days are the most read. Sundays are typically the big day of the week for housing classifieds, but there is usually at least one other day that is popular as well. Focus on those key days if it's cheaper to advertise just on those days than for an entire week.

Look for local (smaller) newspapers that just target your home's area.

Some real estate agents, especially agents that work for larger brokerages, will run ads in the Sunday paper for homes they are listing. These brokerages may get discounts for their ads. Not all agents run these ads, or some may charge you for them. It's certainly better to take advantage of any discount your agent can get than to run the ad on your own. Also keep your ad short and sweet and focus on the most important details, since you'll probably be charged per line. A useful trick is to ad a line of space at the start and the end of your ad, this really separates it from the other ads and draws your potential buyer's eyes to your ad. This is actually more effective than having an ad of the same length but with more details and no blank lines.

Here is a sample of what I mean:

**RENT-TO-OWN**
Oakland Hills, 3 Br/2 Ba. $1250/Mo
(123) 456-7890

This ad would be a total of 5 lines, including the 2 blank ones. It is very simple but it tells your tenant-buyers the key criteria they need to know to get them started. The first is putting rent-to-own in all caps, which lets them know they've found what they are looking for. The second line tells them if the home has enough bedrooms and baths to meet their needs and whether they can afford the monthly rent. The third line tells them how to contact you so they can learn more. Also, depending on where you live in the country, rent-to-own might be more recognized, but there are some other phrases that might be better understood: Lease with Option to Buy, Lease to Own, Rent with Option to Buy, etc. See what works for your area and go with it.

Compare that ad to this 5 line ad:

Rent-to-Own Oakland Hills
3 Br/2 Ba. 1350 Sq Ft.$159,900.
$1250/Mo
Gorgeous Home
(123) 456-7890

This second ad does contain more information, but it get's crammed in and hard to read, plus some of the information just isn't necessary to have in the ad. Rent-to-own buyers are actually less concerned with the asking price than they are with the monthly rent amount (at least initially). The "gorgeous home" line is meant to entice buyers, but when it comes to real estate ads, that really doesn't mean much anymore.

There is another approach you can try with ads as well. A student of mine from Seattle always says he uses "romance" in his ads. For instance, instead of saying:

Nice 3 bdrm home in Seattle.

He might put something like:

> Seattle breathtaking home
> w/view of the water and Mt. Rainier.
> These views can be seen from your
> new hot tub on your deck.
> Call today – this home won't last. $1795/month
> Rent to own available.
> (123) 456-7890

Or:

> Sit by the fireplace in the winter
> w/your sweetheart in this
> 3 brdm home in Seattle. $1295/month
> Rent to own this great home.
> (123) 456-7890

He also has a fun one that I also have used with some success. It sounds odd, but goes like this:

This ad would make people call and say, "What do you mean by FREE PIZZA?" Then we would respond by saying, "Well, when you rent a home with us you get FREE PIZZA every month delivered to your door. Would you like to know more about this home?"

### Signs

If you have your home listed with an agent they'll put a sign in front of the house. Make sure they put a rent-to-own rider on the sign as well. This tells people driving by the house that it's a rent-to-own home. There are many types of these riders. I use the following: Rent-to-Own, Lease Option, Lease or Buy, For Rent (on the top) and For Sale (on the bottom) – etc.

Unless you live on a high-traffic street, one sign in front of your home isn't really going to attract much interest. You can have more signs printed up or better yet, make your own for free. Post several around the area - at the entrance to your subdivision and around some nearby busy streets. Draw buyers to your home. As far as what the sign should say, I would use the same wording as the classified ad above. Most people that are driving by aren't going to have time to read anything more. Plus, if you try to cram too much information on a sign, it won't be readable from a distance. Make sure the sign is big enough to read. Don't simply take an 8 ½ by 11 sheet of paper and put cardboard on the back. That's too small for people driving by to notice. A good size for road-side signs is 1 ½ foot tall by 2 foot wide and use EXTRA LARGE lettering.

*I don't recommend this type of sign. All you have room for is your phone number, and no one will know your home is a rent-to-own. If you try to cram extra information in the little white space it won't be readable, especially to cars driving by.*

## Flyers

Ask your real estate agent to put a flyer box up along with the sign in front of your home. Make sure the flyer has rent-to-own in large lettering on the top. Ask for a bunch of extra copies to keep the box stocked as it runs out. If you don't live in the house anymore, make sure someone keeps it full. The first batch will disappear, mostly from nosey neighbors.

In addition to keeping the flyer box stocked, take some copies and post them around nearby bulletin boards. Laundromats, human resource centers of nearby corporations - especially hospitals, grocery stores, church bulletin boards and even nearby apartment complexes. These are all good places to post flyers.

## Word of Mouth

When you are trying to sell your home, especially on a rent-to-own basis, you should mention it to everyone you know. Your neighbors, your family, your friends, your co-workers, your church, any social organizations you belong to, your mafia don, all of these are great formats to get the word out. The point isn't to mention it just to people you think may be looking for a rent-to-own home; it's to mention it to everyone you know. The reason is that while the person you are telling may not be looking for a new home, they may know someone who is.

*Internet*

The internet is a fantastic marketing tool. Outside of a real estate agent, more and more home buyers are using it as their primary resource for finding a home. As you know, the internet is huge, so you want to make sure you are targeting potential home buyers in your area, not in Nepal. One of my favorites is www.Craigslist.org. It's free to use and you can post your rent-to-own home with pictures. Best of all, it's broken down by areas so you'll be advertising for potential buyers that are looking in your area. Just make sure you delete your old ad and add it as a fresh listing every 3-4 days or every week so it comes up near the top. In addition to posting the ad, www.Craigslist.org also has a discussion forum. Find a discussion for rent-to-owns and mention your home or start your own discussion.

In addition to www.Craigslist.org, I also recommend looking for other local discussion forums. They are free to join and a great place to spread the word. Instead of discussion forums, www.Yahoo.com has groups. Try searching the Yahoo groups for your city name and real estate, such as *Phoenix Real Estate*, that will show you groups relating to the topic where you can post your rent-to-own home.

Also, Google words like *rent to own in San Diego*, *rentals in San Diego*, or *rental home in southern California* (well, if you live there). See what comes up. Those are sites you might want to consider being on.

## Wendy's Wisdom

*Remember, if you are using a real estate agent she may do some of these things for you. As part of your selection process when interviewing real estate agents, you should ask what types of marketing they will do for your home.*

## Create Your Own Website

You can create your own website, or have your neighbor's computer-wizard kid do it for you. Most Internet Service Providers (the company you pay for your internet service) have a certain amount of space allotted for your account to create a website. It's just that VERY few of us ever actually make use of it. Since you are already paying for the internet service, adding the site is free. Include the website in your other advertising, on the flyers, make a rider to go on the sign in your front yard, mention the site when you post in www.Craigslist.org and other forums. You can even add a line to your newspaper classified ad with the website address if you want.

On the website have details about the home, such as the rental rate, the asking price, how many bedrooms and baths and square footage. Emphasize the highlights like recent improvements and whether it has a garage or basement and so on. Include some details such as what school district your home is in and what amenities are close by like shopping, dining and entertainment. You should include a brief description of what rent-to-own is. It can be someone's road to home ownership. I have a one pager in my *Rent-to-Sell* course you can use. Include lots of pictures – make sure the pictures are of the home looking its best. Create a video or slideshow and upload it to your site, if possible.

The purpose of the website is not for people to find it by doing an internet search -- the odds are just too small to consider. The purpose is to get people who found out about your rent-to-own home from other advertising to take a look and get more information.

This is helpful for two reasons. First, many people don't like to call strangers to get information if they aren't sure it's something they are looking for. In other words, the average person reading one of your ads would like to know more about the home and the details before they decide whether to call. By having the website, they can get that information, look at the photos, and then if they are interested, call to view the home.

Secondly, the website helps reduce your call volume to relevant callers. It makes your life easier by not having to answer as many questions from callers who may not be interested in your home. After you have taken 30 or 40 calls from tire-kickers, you will quickly come to appreciate the value of having a website to reduce that call volume. You can place a link to your website at the end of your ad.

## Wendy's Wisdom

*If you have a real estate agent listing your home, you'll want their contact information on the advertising instead of yours (make sure you ask them what needs to be included because they have certain regulations they must follow). That way they are handling the showings and the phone calls, which is one of the services you are paying them for.*

### Marketing for Buyers in Addition to Marketing Your Home

Not every potential buyer knows what rent-to-own is. Many would-be buyers that were rejected for mortgages think they don't have an option for buying a home, so they are stuck renting. If you only advertise your home in one place, you'll never capture the attention of these buyers. It's a good idea to essentially double up on your marketing. When you are posting flyers, joining discussion forums online, and telling people about your home for sale, take the opportunity to also market for buyers. Post ads and flyers that say something like, "Can't qualify for a mortgage? You can still get a home by renting-to-own," or "Bad Credit? You can still own your own home." Give them your phone number (or your agent's phone number) and/or website. When you are spreading the word to people you know about your home being for sale on a rent-to-own basis, tell them that it works great for people who can't qualify for a mortgage or who have poor or bad credit.

## Answer the Phone and Return Calls

This seems like it would be obvious, yet way too often people don't answer their phones or return their calls. People advertise their home for sale or rent, but then don't answer the phone or don't return calls from the messages they receive. This usually happens after the home has been on the market for a while and the seller starts getting tired of answering the same questions over and over again. They start thinking every caller is just another tire kicker, so why bother calling back.

The truth is that MOST of the calls will be tire kickers. Most people won't be interested in your home. But among that group of "most" people is also the ONE person that will buy your home. You'll never get that buyer in your home if you don't take all of those other calls as well. Use a phone that will get answered. This is probably your cell phone.

### Wendy's Wisdom

*Remember, if you are using a real estate agent to sell your home you don't have to take these calls. Your advertising should have your real estate agent's number. This makes your life so much easier.*

In the next section we'll be focusing on the paperwork particular to rent-to-own transactions. Understanding this paperwork will help you tremendously when it comes to receiving an offer and negotiating your sale. I won't try to make you an expert in contracts because you won't need to be one to sell your home on a rent-to-own basis. Having a solid understanding of the paperwork can often make a difference of thousands of dollars in the end, so you definitely want to read these next chapters. In the next few chapters, I will assume you have the contracts from my website. If you don't have them and you started with this book, I recommend getting them by the time you sell your home to someone as a rent-to-own.

# PART 3:

## UNDERSTANDING THE PAPERWORK

# Chapter 8

## Rental Agreements

Okay, here comes the fun part: the paperwork! No seriously, it is not that complex or scary, but it can seem overwhelming if you don't take it one piece at a time. This process of rent-to-own can seem a bit complex, so I'll try to keep it simple. There are many ideas and suggestions in this book for those who want every detail. Some do, some don't. Some will go through it all, some won't. It is here so you can use what works for you, and what you feel comfortable with. In this chapter, I refer to the *tenant* as the *buyer* and you are the *owner*, or *landlord*. Let's dig right in.

### The Basics

The *rental agreement* (a.k.a. lease agreement) is basically an agreement between you and the tenant-buyer that defines the terms of the rental period. These are the basic points it covers:

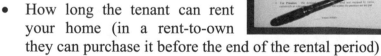

- How long the tenant can rent your home (in a rent-to-own they can purchase it before the end of the rental period)
- What they will pay each month for their rental payment
- Where and how they will pay you
- How much and where you will hold their security deposit
- Any other provisions such as late fees, bounced checks, rental agreement violations, etc.
- And, of course, the required Lead Based Paint language

## Fill in the Blanks

It isn't necessary to go over a rental agreement in detail because you don't need to know every detail to rent your home.

Most good rental agreements take the guesswork out of the picture for you, making your life significantly easier. They do this by having all of the regular terms and conditions pre-printed. When it comes to completing the details that are specific to YOUR rental, you simply fill in the blanks. You will fill in how long the rental agreement lasts, how much the monthly rent is and security deposit, and so forth.

## Wendy's Wisdom

*You should never draft your own rental agreements (or any other contracts for that matter) from scratch. Always use pre-created contracts (preferably pro-seller) and just fill in the relevant details. Creating your own can cause you enormous headaches and potential legal problems.*

## Pro-Seller vs. Neutral

Not all paperwork and contracts are created equally. What I mean by this is I have contracts that protect me, or my clients, when I am selling, but I have different ones to protect me when I am buying. I call these my "pro-seller" and "pro-buyer" contracts. You, as the seller, will want pro-seller contracts for your transaction. You can order these on my website if you don't already have them.

In fact, there are three different types of contracts: Pro-Seller, Neutral, and Pro-Buyer. Obviously, you want the ones that are pro-seller. They offer you the most protection and the most favorable terms.

You usually do NOT want to accept the rental agreement from a buyer or the buyer's agent. They will be, AT BEST, neutral.

You are the one leasing out your home. You get to choose which rental agreement to use. If the buyer has an issue with any of the terms of your rental agreement, you can always negotiate. I can't think of one case, in my hundreds of rent-to-own transactions, where the buyer questioned the rental agreement I was using. If they wanted the house, they signed my paperwork. You can also use my pro-seller clauses and just add those to their contract.

## Wendy's Wisdom

*Not all contracts are the same. Protect yourself by making sure you have pro-seller contracts – even if you are working with a real estate agent.*

You also don't want to use the rental agreement your real estate agent has (unless they have mine), as they typically have only one set of contracts and they are usually neutral. If you chose to work with a real estate agent when selling your home on a rent-to-own basis, you can still use the contracts you get from my website as they will be much more favorable to you (or update the agent's contracts with my clauses to protect you).

### How Much of a Difference Can it Make for You?

Here is just one example. If you use a real estate agent that has a limited understanding of rent-to-own and use their paperwork, you may in fact, end up having all of your paperwork combined into one contract. If the tenant stopped paying the rent and you tried to evict, you would be very unhappy to find that the judge may not let you evict, because of the nature of your paperwork. The judge may consider your transaction a sale instead of a rental and require you to foreclose.

In Michigan for example, it takes an EXTRA 6 to 9 months to foreclose. If your monthly mortgage payment is $1,200 per month you are talking about $7,200 to $10,800!

## Key Clauses

Here are several of the clauses you will find in my rental agreements that make them pro-seller.

## Co-Signer

If you have a weak applicant, a co-signer can be an important safeguard. The co-signer is someone who will not be living in the home but is agreeing to be responsible for the rent each month. The co-signer should have a strong income and good credit. Co-signers are typically parents, but can sometimes be close friends or other family members. I love co-signers. They make good money and have strong credit, so you know you'll get paid.

The key thing about having a co-signer for a weak applicant (which may be the situation your tenant-buyer is in) is you can hold the co-signer responsible if the applicant stops paying rent or bounces rent checks.

*Celebrating Parents –*

*Some parents will be happy to cosign if they can finally get their kids to move out of the house.*

## *Initial Every Page*

At the bottom of EVERY page of the rental agreement I have a spot for the tenant and you (the seller) to initial. You do this in addition to signing the end of the rental agreement because it leaves no room for doubt that the whole rental agreement was agreed to and signed by the tenant. That way, if there ever comes a time when you have to enforce a section of the rental agreement and the tenant says, "I never agreed to that!" you just show them the rental agreement with their initials on it.

### *Late Rent Can Make it Month-to-Month*

*This Rental Agreement can revert to a month to month agreement if the tenant becomes more than 10 days late on any option payment or rental payment, at the written discretion of the landlord.*

If the tenant-buyer pays their rent more than 10 days late, you can convert the lease to a month-to-month tenancy. By reverting to month-to-month you can then give the tenant 1 month notice to vacate and re-advertise your home to place another tenant-buyer.

*Note: You would only want to do this if you no longer want to sell your home to that tenant-buyer.*

### *Late Rent (10 days) Can Void the Option*

One useful clause is to give you, the seller, the right to invalidate the option agreement if the tenant pays the rent more than 10 days late. You don't have to enforce it and probably won't because the goal is to sell your home. However, should the tenant become undesirable, it allows you to discontinue the tenancy after the tenant is late on a payment by 10 days. I have this in my rental agreement, but have only used it one time over the last 20+ years. Of course, you will also get a late fee if they are late on their rent payment.

### How Payments Will Be Applied

This is a great clause. It specifies the order in which a tenant's payments will be applied should they have other charges or fees due besides rent:

1. Outstanding dishonored check fees

2. Outstanding late fees chargeable to tenant

3. Outstanding legal fees, court costs or both

4. Outstanding utility bills that are the tenant's responsibility

5. Any damage caused by tenant

6. Collection agency fees

7. Costs for re-letting the property, if applicable

8. Option fees owed (confirm this with your attorney first – you might not want to mention anything about the option fee in the rental agreement. It will depend on where you live)

9. And lastly, for rent

You can see that rent comes last on the list, with good reason. This is because it is much easier to evict for unpaid rent than it is for any other unpaid charges. As bills come up, document them on your tenant payment ledger and make sure the payments you receive get applied the same way. Send your tenant any updates on the statement.

### Assignments and Subletting

*Resident/Tenant shall not assign this Agreement or sublet any portion of the premises without prior written consent of the Owner.*

Do not let tenants sublet or rent ANY portion of your home without your consent. That person's name is not on the rental agreement and you don't have the same enforcement rights over that person.

Do not allow the option or rental agreement to be assigned to someone else without your consent. You need to be able to screen that person just the same as you screened your tenant-buyer.

If you do agree to an assignment or sublet you definitely want to get that person to sign a new contract.

**Entry and Inspection**

*Resident/Tenant shall permit Owner or Owner's agent to enter the premises at reasonable times and upon reasonable notice for the purpose of inspecting the premises or showing the same to prospective tenants or purchasers, or for making necessary repairs.*

This gives you the right to enter the property at reasonable times and with reasonable notice to inspect the home. This is not to allow you to inspect the tenant's personal life, but instead to allow you to make sure that the home and property are being maintained in accordance with the terms of the rental agreement. Remember, they don't own the home yet. If they are not choosing to purchase the home, you want to have the right to place a new "for sale" sign on the front lawn and conduct showings. You will have to notify them of any scheduled showings with due notice.

## Wendy's Wisdom

*You should NOT even step onto the lawn without calling the tenant first. This is violating their "rights to peaceful enjoyment". Just because it's your home doesn't give you the right to stop by anytime. Call and ask if it is okay. You do have the right as an owner to come by, but only with reasonable notice. In my area it is important to give a 24-hour notice unless there is an emergency (fire, flood, etc.).*

## Ordinances and Statutes

*Resident/Tenant shall comply with all statutes, ordinances and requirements of all municipal, state and federal authorities now in force, or which may hereafter be in force, pertaining to the use of the premises. Owner/Landlord has the right to immediate eviction of resident/tenant for any illegal activity on the premises.*

The tenant must abide by local zoning laws for usage of the property. For example, they can't run a daycare business in the home if it isn't zoned properly (there is also another clause about business use of the home). You have the right, as the landlord, to evict immediately for any illegal operations on the premises such as running a brothel or manufacturing and/or selling drugs.

## Waiver

*Failure of the Owner to enforce any term hereof shall not constitute a waiver, nor shall acceptance of a partial payment of rent or other money claim be deemed a waiver of the Owner's right to the full amount due and owing.*

For example if I waive the late fee one month or don't enforce the late fee one month that doesn't negate my right to enforce it the next month.

In the next chapter we will look at the option agreement. This is the contract that reserves the right for the tenant-buyer to purchase your home at a later date.

# Chapter 9

## Option Agreements

The option agreement gives the tenant-buyer the right to buy your home at a later date. It is binding only to the seller, meaning that the option agreement prevents the seller from selling the home to anyone else as long as the option is valid. The tenant-buyer is not obligated to buy the home. However, it does set some terms and conditions upon which the option may become invalid and release you, the seller, to sell your home to someone else.

### The Basics

The option agreement is really fairly simple and short. These are the basic points it covers:

- The amount of the option fee
- When and how it will be paid
- The date range during which the option is valid
- Whether there will be any additional option credits
- A very clear statement that their option fee is non-refundable if they choose not to purchase the home

- A statement on who will cover repairs or expenses during the option period.

## What the Option Agreement Doesn't Contain

Almost as important as what it does contain is what it doesn't contain. It is important to keep the option distinct and separate from both the rental agreement and the sales contract. Along those lines the option agreement usually does not contain any details about the purchase price. Those details are contained in the sales contract. It does not contain any details about financing. It also doesn't contain details about the rental agreement. Each of these contracts is separate for a reason.

## Wendy's Wisdom

*It is important to have a separate and distinct option agreement from other paperwork. The option agreement should not contain any details about the purchase price, financing or rental details.*

***Note:*** *In some cases it can be combined with a sales contract but never with the rental agreement. The rental agreement is always separate.*

## Fill in the Blanks

Like the rental agreement, the option agreement should have all of the standard information pre-printed. This leaves you only with the responsibility of filling in the blanks that are specifically pertinent to your home. You would fill in such blanks as who the optionor (you) and who the optionee (tenant-buyer) are. Other key points you would also fill in would be the amount of the option fee and the date range the option is valid. Don't try to draft up a whole option agreement or any other paperwork on your own. I guarantee you will miss a lot of essential details.

**Pro-Seller vs. Neutral**

Like the rental agreement, option contracts can be pro-seller, neutral or pro-buyer. Believe me, it makes a difference!

Your best bet would be to use the contracts from my website. I have been using them and improving on them for more than twenty years. If you elect not to purchase them I would recommend you retain the services of an attorney to help you get the most protection possible. Sign up at www.PrepaidLegal.com/hub/wendypatton to get the best rates and advice.

I absolutely do NOT recommend that you just make use of the contracts your real estate agent has. As I said before, they will be neutral at best.

## Wendy's Wisdom

*I cannot stress how important it is to get help. Use pro-seller contracts to help you with your paperwork. Use a real estate agent or an attorney to assist you with the sale of your home. It will make your life so much easier.*

**Key Clauses**

Here are several of the clauses you will find in my option agreement that make them pro-seller. Remember the optionee is the tenant-buyer and you (the seller) are the optionor.

## As-Is

*Optionee is agreeing to accept the property in "as-is" condition.*

This protects you. It means the tenant-buyer is buying the home in whatever condition it is in. This does not exclude you from proper disclosure, however. You still must disclose known defects in the home.

## Repairs

*Optionee agrees to make all repairs major and minor to the property.*

This clause can save you a TON of money during the rental and option period. This keeps you from being obligated to make repairs on your home during the rental period.

It isn't as simple as just leaving this clause in your contract and not doing any repairs if they are needed. The tenant-buyer is still, technically a tenant. When you are a tenant (renter) you usually can be held responsible for a small deductable for a repair (in most states), but not major repairs. That would normally be addressed in the rental agreement. In a rent-to-own situation you will never want to mention large repairs or all repairs in a rental agreement. The option agreement can contain language about repairs. You can't treat them 100% like an owner unless you want to do seller financing and transfer title to them (that is another technique and another book). I have a clause that basically states they are responsible for the repairs or assessments on the home during the option period, but if I have to do any of them, I will add it to the purchase price, plus a small interest rate (make sure it is a legal interest rate).

## Septic

*If there is a septic system, the optionee agrees to have it pumped once per year.*

For those of you that don't know what septic is - ☺ it is the waste disposal system for a home that is not tied to a city sewer system. If you live out in the country or on larger lots, you might have one of these. I do. Proper maintenance is very important and you don't want to have to pay for it.

## Assessments

*Optionor should pay for all additional assessments, including water, sewage, sidewalks and road paving.*

If you have any additional assessments levied against your home during the option period, they are the responsibility of the tenant-buyer. I addressed this in the previous paragraph on repairs.

## Equitable Mortgage

*This option to purchase is not, and shall not be construed as, or interpreted as any form of equitable mortgage. It is hereby declared that it is not the intent of the parties to create a loan of any nature or to create a mortgage of any kind. In the event that the optionee hereunder should ever raise such an issue in a court of law or otherwise, this option shall terminate immediately.*

*Oh, the dreaded Equitable Mortgage!*

*Equitable mortgage* simply means the person on the buying end of the contract has "equity". The reason this becomes important is IF things don't go well with your tenant-buyer and you have to evict them, some judges might look at the option as "equitable mortgage" or "equitable title," which is why we have this clause. Either way, this determination would require you, the owner, to foreclose on your tenant-buyer vs. evict them. Foreclosure is much more expensive and time consuming than an eviction. We want to prevent this situation as much as possible.

## Wendy's Wisdom

*An equitable mortgage clause is reason enough to make sure you have pro-seller contracts. Not having one can easily cost you thousands of dollars if you have to foreclose versus evict.*

This is more likely if your home is in California. I always say, "California is like a different country." It is much more pro-tenant. I have a special clause for those of you in California drafted by a California attorney. You will want to use a clause like this to help avoid this situation. It is very rare, but it can happen. Our goal together is to minimize your risks and maximize your benefits. If you live in California, once you buy my contracts you can email my office at support@wendypatton.com to receive this clause.

**Credit Repair Services**

*Optionee agrees to start credit repair services immediately at www.renttoowncreditrepair.com (or wherever you want them to go).*

I suggest you take the money out of the option fee and pay for the credit repair services. This would mean you would only give them credit for the amount they paid less the cost of credit repair. For example if they had $4000 down and credit repair is $800, you would give them credit for $3200 as their option fee they paid you. They would not get credit for the $800 which went to the credit repair.

**Seek Advice (Another CYA Clause)**

*CYA – Cover Your ASSets.* Throughout all of the contracts we want to CYA. In the case of "seek advice" here is what I use:

*The optionor has advised the optionee to seek the advice of a mortgage lender and attorney prior to signing this document.*

It is definitely in your best interest for the tenant-buyer to meet with a mortgage lender (this should have been part of your tenant-buyer screening). You want to make sure they'll be able to qualify for a mortgage down the road. To protect yourself, this clause also advises they seek the advice of an attorney. They will rarely talk to an attorney.

## Wendy's Wisdom

*Do the contracts seem intimidating to you? Remember, your real estate agent and your Pre-Paid Legal attorney can help you. This takes most of the burden off your shoulders.*

I would also like you to consider adding this clause:

*Optionee agrees to start credit repair services.*

That covers the option agreement. In the next chapter we will look at the sales contract, which defines the terms and conditions for the tenant-buyer to purchase your home.

# Chapter 10

## Sales Contract

The sales contract is sometimes called *Offer to Purchase, Purchase Contract, Purchase Sales Contract, Sales Agreement* or a multitude of similar things. The most common one is the *Sales Contract*. This contract outlines and details the terms and conditions of the sale of your home. In this chapter your tenant-buyer will be called the *purchaser* and you are the *seller*.

**The Basics**

These are the basic points the sales contract covers:

1.     The agreed upon purchase price.

2.     Any personal property that will come with the sale of the home (for instance any appliances or anything not attached to the home).

3.     If there will be an inspection and what the conditions of the inspection will be.

4.     What type of financing will be used to purchase the home. In the case of your agreement you do not want any financing contingencies in the sales contract.

5.     What type of title insurance will be provided and who will pay.

6.  In some states there are very specific clauses that must go in your sales contract (California has many).

7.  If there is a real estate broker involved there will be clauses about their role and exclusion from liability for the entire transaction.

## What it Doesn't Contain

The sales contract usually does not contain anything about what amount was put down as an option fee. This is only in the option agreement. I do not recommend it in a sales contract, otherwise it will appear to be an *earnest deposit*, which is refundable in certain circumstances. I want to make sure it is clear that the option fee is only referenced in the option  agreement. It doesn't mention the dates of when the offer (sales contract) is valid. It only refers to "See attached option agreement signed this same day."

## Wendy's Wisdom

*The sales contract does not contain any reference to the option fee or when the option to purchase is valid. Doing so may turn the option fee into an earnest deposit, which can become refundable to the buyer if they choose not to or cannot buy.*

## Fill in the Blanks

Much of the sales contract is standard, but you will need to fill in some information. Of course you will need the price, the property legal description and the address. This is the main part of what you fill in.

**Pro-Seller**

Like the other agreements, sales contracts can be either pro-seller, neutral or pro-buyer. It makes a difference.

Again, your best bet would be to use the contracts you purchase from my website or use your state approved contract, and add the pro-seller statements from my contract into your state contract. I have been using them and improving on them for more than twenty years. If you elect not to purchase them, I would recommend you retain the services of an attorney to help you get the most protection possible. Remember also, the most cost effective way to obtain legal advice is through Pre-Paid Legal, which you can enroll at www.PrepaidLegal.com/hub/wendypatton. They can review these contracts at no charge and give you recommendations. The best way to go is to use an expert's contracts (mine) and an attorney in your state to review.

A few states now have mandatory sales contracts, meaning you must use the state approved contract. If your state requires using a specific contract, you will need to add addendums to that sales contract for it to work in a rent-to-own situation.

**Key Clauses**

Here are several of the clauses you will find in my sales agreement that make it pro-seller.

*As-Is*

*Purchasers understand that they are purchasing a USED structure in an 'AS IS' condition. The Purchaser acknowledges that: (a)they have examined the property; and (b) they have had the opportunity to have additional inspections.*

I have this in the *option agreement* as well. I want to make sure it is very clear. Purchaser is agreeing to accept the property in "as-is" condition. This is key to keep you out of trouble if something goes wrong later with the home.

You will have to fill out a "property condition statement", "seller's disclosure", or whatever you state calls it, to detail the condition of your home. You MUST disclose the condition of the home and not leave anything out. Selling your home in as-is condition does not circumvent the need for disclosure.

For instance, if I had a basement that leaked at one time, I must disclose it. If I state my basement doesn't leak and later they find out it did before (from the neighbors or someone) then I could be liable for the next leak even if I fixed it the first time. The best way to protect yourself is to over-disclose items on your home. For that basement instance, I would state that my basement did leak before, but I have fixed it to the best of my knowledge. This way, when the tenant-buyer signs that disclosure form, they are aware of the situation. The same goes for roof leaks, pests, etc.

## Wendy's Wisdom

*I can't stress enough – disclose, disclose, disclose. When in doubt, disclose. Okay? That should be clear now.*

### Property Inspection

*The Purchasers may have the physical condition, structural, plumbing, heating, and electrical systems of the property inspected by a contractor of his own choice within _____ days from the date of acceptance of this offer and at his own expense. If seller does not receive written notice from the purchaser(s) of their dissatisfaction regarding said inspection within 3 days from date of inspection, this contingency will be considered satisfied and the purchase agreement is binding without regard to said report. If the seller does receive written notice, within the time provided, that purchaser(s) are dissatisfied, purchaser(s) at their election may terminate this agreement and all deposited monies shall be returned to purchaser(s). If purchaser moves into the property, all rights to a property inspection will be waived and purchaser will be accepting the property "as is".*

Purchaser signs off whether they will or will not have an inspection. Do NOT let them move in without doing this first! Meaning if they choose not to do one, that is fine, BUT I still have them sign off on it that they have personally done it and are satisfied with the results.

What you don't want is for them to move in without signing off on the inspection and a month later say, "We want to move out because the furnace isn't working right," or something minor like that. If someone has buyer's remorse or personal financial issues they will think of anything to get out and try to get their money back. You want to make sure your contracts are tight and pro-seller.

### *Default*

*In the event of default by Purchaser, Seller may, at his option, declare a forfeiture thereunder and retain the deposit. In the event of default by Seller, Purchaser may, at his option, demand, and be entitled to, an immediate refund of his entire option deposit in full termination of this Agreement.*

If the purchaser defaults they lose their option fee. If you, the seller, default you must give them their option fee back.

For instance, something happens to you which prevents you from selling for a period of time, and the buyer wants to buy - now. They are entitled to sue you for specific performance (meaning you must sell them the home), unless there is another provision in the sales contract for excluding specific performance for something outside of your control. For instance, you get divorced and your ex-spouse decides to sue you and it shows up on the title of the home and is refusing to sign for the closing (divorce doesn't always make people react rationally).

For the most part, you should not be in default. Make sure you make your mortgage payments, and don't get into financial trouble elsewhere jeopardizing your purchaser's position. This would not be good for anyone.

## Title Insurance

*Seller agrees to pay for title insurance for purchaser at the time of closing. If seller can not get title insurance for the home, then seller can either return any option fees obtained as full and complete liquidated damages (and call this offer null and void) or the seller may remedy the title problem, whichever seller chooses, or the purchaser may elect to accept the title 'AS IS'.*

This clause describes what type of title insurance you will give your buyer. There are "attorney states" and "title company states". If you are in an attorney state you will need to find a title attorney to do the title work and they perform the closing as well. If you are in a title insurance state, you will need to locate a title insurance company.

Either way, you don't have to know too much about this. Your real estate agent can suggest a title attorney/title company or the mortgage lender for the buyer will pick one. They will know who is good.

In many states, the fees are regulated. You can ask your agent or the buyer's lender if this is the case in your state. If they are regulated, the costs will be pretty much the same no matter who you use. If they are not regulated, feel free to shop around and to get the best deal. Some might vary, especially if they are attorney-controlled. However, bear in mind that the lowest price isn't always the best deal if the quality of service is lousy. Remember, you are selling your home, not bargain hunting for Christmas sales.

### Other Conditions

This is where you would put additional specific items that belong in this contract. For instance, real estate agents must disclose they are an agent if they are a buyer or seller of a property. If you are a licensed real estate agent you need to put that in writing.

I also put in this section some of the option agreement clauses on repairs and how they will be added to the purchase price at closing. I want no confusion on this and want all parties to be very clear on how this will be handled. I also have the buyer sign off on the same statement as in the option agreement about them contacting an attorney and mortgage lender prior to signing this document.

Also, I include a statement that says:

*Purchaser had the home inspected on* _____ *and they are satisfied with the results and are purchasing the home "AS IS."*

In the blank you will have them insert the day they inspected the home or their inspector inspected it. I think I beat this inspection clause and "AS IS" clause to death, but I want no confusion from either side down the road.

That covers the sales contract. In the next chapter we will look at the *memorandum of option*, which you generally will not want to use, but I am sharing the information with you in case you choose to do so or need it for your purchaser to get a mortgage.

# Chapter 11

# Memorandum of Option

The *memorandum of option* is a document that gives the world notice of the option you are giving to your tenant-buyer. It is a questionable document for a seller, as far as benefit, to sign and record, so don't jump right in with it. If you were a buyer and I was consulting you, I would definitely recommend it, but not so much for a seller.

You don't need to read this chapter unless you have worked with the lender for your tenant-buyer and they have requested you use this document or the tenant-buyer is insisting on having it (very unlikely unless they read my book for buyers). The mortgage industry is changing daily and they might prefer this be recorded at some point. This is pretty much the only time you would use this document.

## Wendy's Wisdom

*The memorandum of option is NOT required in a rent-to-own transaction. As a seller you don't necessarily need it or want it.*

### The Basics

*What it Contains*

These are the basic points it covers:

- When the option is valid
- Who the parties are
- Legal description and address of the property

(so that it can be recorded)
- Sometimes it could contain other provisions (mostly if you are a buyer)

### What it Doesn't Contain

It doesn't contain anything about the details of the transaction. It doesn't usually contain any financial numbers about rental amounts or purchase price.

### Fill in the Blanks

The major things you need to fill in are:

- The dates of the option
- The names of the parties involved
- The address and legal description of the property
- Where to mail the document when it is recorded against the title

### Pro-Seller?

This is really a pro-buyer document, for the most part. Once you file a memorandum on a property, you, as the seller, can't:

- Sell to anyone else (or)
- Refinance the property

These are things you shouldn't do anyway during the rental period. Your tenant-buyer might not be too happy if you sell your home to someone else while they are living in it.

The other reason the memorandum of option is disadvantageous to you, the seller, is if for some reason the buyer defaults during the option period you will have to make sure the memorandum gets removed properly. In other words, the cloud it puts on your title must be lifted so you can resell your home again.

An eviction would do this in most states, but if someone were to leave in the middle of the night (sorry, that has happened before) then it might take some work and money to get it off of your title. I really don't recommend it unless you are working with a lender that requires it to do the loan for your buyer. Only use it for that purpose, meaning the lending requirements are such that it will be helpful to get your buyer to the closing table.

## Wendy's Wisdom

*Remember-- your goal is to sell your home. If you need a memorandum of option to achieve that goal, then do it.*

### Requirements

This is the only document that you will sign with your tenant-buyer that is notarized. A document must be notarized to be recorded in all states that I am aware of.

None of this matters at all if you see no reason to use this document. If you need one, there is one included in my *Rent-to-Sell* course.

That covers the *memorandum of option*. In the next chapter we will look at the key points to negotiate before you complete these contracts with your tenant-buyer.

# PART 4

## RECEIVING AN OFFER
## AND NEGOTIATIONS

# Chapter 12

## Key Points to Negotiate – Not all deals are created equal

Rent-to-own transactions have more points to negotiate than most real estate transactions. Although, all real estate transactions have more points to negotiate than you probably ever knew. While this might seem complicated, in actuality it gives you more ways to work around points that your tenant-buyer is stuck on. In other words, if your tenant-buyer is fixated on a specific rental rate, you can negotiate to your benefit in other areas to accommodate them such as a higher purchase price. If they are fixated on the pool table in your basement you can ask for them to pay for your daughter's wedding.

Life is all about negotiating. Think about a two year old. They ask for another cookie. You say, "No." They ask again. You say, "No." They start to pout and ask again. You say, "No." Then they start to cry. This can go on and on. Now what do you do?

Some of us would say, "Go to your room now or sit in that corner because you are not getting another cookie." Some of us might say, "Fine, here is the cookie, but no more." And

*The world's most effective negotiating technique!*

some of us would say, "Okay, you can have another cookie after your nap." The two year old is negotiating with his parent and sometimes he will win! All of us, in some way, like to negotiate.

Many home buyers and sellers think that price and closing cost are the only negotiating points for them to buy or sell a home. There are more negotiating points than price and the more of them you know the stronger your negotiating advantage is. We'll get into some of the HOWS of negotiating in the next chapter. Here we will focus on WHAT to negotiate.

## Wendy's Wisdom

*Remember, a real estate agent can help you with negotiations. Real estate agents also deal in submitting offers and counter-offers, so you don't have to negotiate face-to-face with your buyers. This gives you time to check back in this book for items to negotiate in case you forget something.*

### *Price*

Price, of course, is the big one that most everyone focuses on. In rent-to-own, sales price gets a little more complicated because the sale takes place over time. This means that the value of your home may increase or decrease during the course of the rental period, depending on your real estate market.

As the home seller, you are typically able to ask for a rent-to-own price premium, meaning you can ask a little more than market value because you are offering the home on a rent-to-own basis. The stronger the real estate market, the greater the premium you can ask for. Remember, however, if you ask for too much you may not find a tenant-buyer, or it may take you a long time to find a tenant-buyer. In most cases price is not what is important to the tenant-buyer, the other terms are.

If you are living in a market that is appreciating right now, you will want to take into account some or all of the market appreciation in determining the price as well as the price premium. You might want to give your tenant-buyers some of the appreciation, but it's only fair that you should get part of it as well. This usually is factored in as part of your price premium. That's why stronger markets get higher rent-to-own price premiums than weaker markets. The range I use is 5-10% (in stronger markets), depending on the comparables in the area and how strong the market is.

However, if the sale is going to take place more than 12 to 18 months down the road, you may want to add price increases over time. What I mean is you can have built-in price increases in your contract over a period of time. If your current selling price is $150,000 you can make that valid for a period of 12 to 18 months. Then you can have the price go up to, say, $155,000 if the tenant-buyer purchases within 24 months or $165,000 if they buy within 36 months. It depends on your market and how it looks like your home will appreciate in value.

## Wendy's Wisdom

*You don't want to start long term or they will not focus on credit repair or getting a mortgage. They will most likely procrastinate. Use extensions later when they are needed.*

You can also have the price increases come with extensions instead of building extra time into the contract initially. If you only make the option valid for 18 months but then the tenant-buyers need more time and ask for an extension, you can increase the price as part of the extension. Be fair, but also do what works for you. This can work a little better for you because when the tenant-buyer asks for an extension it will be close to when the existing option is going to expire. That means you'll have a better idea of what your real estate market has done, and can make your price increase more accurate, based on the current market.

## *Monthly Rent*

There is some "wiggle room" on the monthly rental rates, but it will depend on your neighborhood. In most areas you'll find that the market rents are set, due to competition. However, in areas with fewer rentals you may see more flexibility.

Most sellers try to determine their rental rate based on their mortgage payment instead of what the rental rate should be. This is a critical mistake that might leave your home sitting on the market for a longer period of time. I know you want to cover that monthly nut you have, but you might not be able to cover 100% of it with market rent. The rent you receive and should charge should be market rent. I covered this in detail in Chapter 5: Pricing and Rental Rates.

Nonetheless, however you set your monthly rent, this is merely the starting asking price, much like the purchase price. It may be negotiated down by the tenant-buyer. Although in some cases you may be able to negotiate it UP based on other things the tenant-buyer asks for.

## How Can You Negotiate a Higher Rent?

### *To offset buyer option credits*

For example, if they ask for a large monthly option credit because they really want to build their equity, to help make the purchase, you can agree, but ask that some of that option credit be reflected in a higher rental rate. Also, if they have less down for their option fee, you might want to increase the monthly rental payment slightly.

### Tack on monthly expenses

If your home has other monthly expenses such as pool maintenance or a lawn service, you can deduct that from what you ask for in monthly rent. This will increase interest in your home based on the lower rental rate. Then, add those as additional fees the tenant-buyer needs to pay. People would rather see a monthly rent of $1425 than $1500, and then add in the $75 per month lawn service. You still end up at $1500, but it sounds better when they are considering what they want to pay in rent.

### Option Fee

The option fee is the amount the tenant-buyer puts down in order to have the exclusive right to buy your home. The option fee is non-refundable. The option fee will depend both on what your tenant-buyers are able to come up with, but also on how much you are willing to accept.

Additionally, stronger markets typically allow you to require larger option fees than weaker markets. For a general rule of thumb and what I have seen across the country, tenant-buyers will have 3-5% of the purchase price in a strong market and 1-2% in a buyer's market. You are most likely in a buyer's market right now and should not expect much more than 1-2%. Can you find more? Maybe.

**Example:** Your asking price for your home is $200,000 – you can expect $2,000 – $4,000 for their option fee. If you get 10% down, $20,000, then jump up and down, dance, sing praises to God and be nice to those tenant-buyers. It is rare!

## Wendy's Wisdom

*Remember, the option fee is NOT the same as the security deposit. The security deposit, if you choose to collect it, would be additional and separate from the option fee.*

One option is to scale option fees based on the credit-worthiness of your tenant-buyers. We'll talk more about credit and screening in Chapter 14. A tenant-buyer with better credit is less of a risk for you, so you might be willing to accept a smaller option fee versus someone who has poor credit, and will have a harder time qualifying for a mortgage down the road. Of course, if they have bad credit they usually don't have much cash (well, they shouldn't have otherwise they should pay their bills). Option fees for a rent-to-own usually apply against the purchase price when the tenant-buyer buys your home, but are non-refundable if they choose not to buy. Keep this in mind when negotiating. Assume that the tenant-buyer will complete the purchase and their option fee will apply against the purchase price. That means the option fee is not "bonus" money, it comes off what you'll receive at the time the sale is completed.

**Your Goal** → SOLD

**Remember your Goal:
Get your home SOLD!**

This can get confusing to some sellers. They think they have to bring this option fee to closing to give the tenant-buyer credit for it. You don't have to bring it to closing, but you will give a payoff letter or a balance due letter indicating you received the money to the tenant-buyer's mortgage lender. The larger the option fee you can collect the better, because it means the tenant-buyer is less likely to walk away from it.

### *Option Credits*

These are amounts during the rental period that are deducted from the end purchase price if the tenant-buyer purchases your home. If they do not purchase, these amounts essentially disappear. Like the option fee, it's not something the tenant-buyer is entitled to if they don't buy. Option credits are in no way required. In some cases, for you as the seller, you would not want to mention them or include them in any offers unless the tenant-buyer asks for them. Most tenant-buyers don't know what they are. You would not want to mention them if you have no equity in your home, and by giving credits you would have to bring money to the closing table. You do want to mention them if you do have equity, and can give some of it up to the tenant-buyer and, it will help get them to buy.

Unless you negotiated a higher rent or higher purchase price for them, option credits are basically free giveaways on your part as an incentive to the tenant-buyer. This does not mean you should not give it to them, but make sure it works for you. The more they have as a credit before the option period is over, the more likely they will purchase your home. How badly do you want to sell your home?

Option credits can be structured in different ways. The simplest way is to have an amount from the monthly rental payment apply as an option credit each month and the amount can vary to whatever you agree to. Instead of having the option credit be the same every month, you can stagger these amounts with smaller option credits in the beginning and more towards the end to help motivate the tenant-buyer or vice versa.

You can also use them as an inducement for things like paying the rent on time, keeping the house properly maintained and so forth. You can do this by including in the option agreement that the tenant-buyer would receive, say, a $1500 option credit at the end of the option period if they have on-time rental payments every month. You can also REVERSE option credits if the tenant-buyer goes beyond the option period and requests an extension. For example, if the tenant-buyer accumulated $4500 in option credits ($250 month) over an 18 month option, but then requested an extension, you could reduce the option credit by some amount for each month over the initial 18 months. This is a good way to effectively increase your purchase price without ASKING for a higher purchase price, which can be very effective if your home hasn't appreciated in value during the option period.

## Wendy's Wisdom

*Reversing option credits, in other words decreasing accumulated option credits, can be a good way to increase your effective selling price when a tenant-buyer asks for an extension.*

### Repairs

Depending on the condition of your home, repairs can either be a large expense or a small expense. The larger the potential expense, the more you'll want to negotiate to protect yourself on this. You can either pay for them all yourself or have the tenant-buyer pay for them all. Or you can do something in between. If the tenant-buyer is going to be paying for the repairs you'll want to ensure that the work is done properly, we talked about this in Chapters 8 and 9 as part of the rental and option agreement.

Another possibility is to offer option credits for repairs that the tenant-buyer pays for. This keeps you from paying out of pocket. In this case we are talking about repairs that the seller would normally pay for, not the ones the tenant-buyer chooses to do.

Remember, also, that my contracts are worded such that any repairs the seller pays for are added to the purchase price, plus interest, when the tenant-buyer buys. It's better to have contracts worded this way than to bring the point up as a negotiating issue.

That way the tenant-buyer is more likely to just accept it instead of bargaining.

The old saying goes, "If it looks like a duck, quacks like a duck, walks like a duck, it's a duck!

### *Property Taxes*

Your property taxes should be physically paid by you even if you "roll it in" to the monthly rent to cover them. I would not call it taxes or mention that to the tenant-buyer. While they are still a tenant-buyer, you do not want to make them cover owner- and landlord-type expenses. If anything were to go wrong with you, and the tenant-buyer and a judge got involved, they would not look kindly towards you on this type of arrangement. The court would interpret this as a sale of your property despite calling it a rent-to-own.

What this means is; if you make it look like a sale rather than a rent-to-own you could put yourself in a situation that, when things don't go well (i.e. you have to evict a tenant-buyer) a judge might make you go through foreclosure versus an eviction. As I have said before you do not want to do this, as it is much longer and costlier to do a foreclosure than an eviction.

In some states and areas you might hear of *equitable interest*. This is when you give your tenant-buyer too much equity or too much responsibility that it looks like a sale versus a rental agreement. There is a fine line on this situation, and in most cases would never come up (unless you live in California).

Seriously, there are some states, like California, where consumers have more rights, and it is harder for business people. You are now the "business" and you want to be careful, and do things right. I don't want you to become paranoid, but I do want you to be smart.

## Special Assessments

Tax assessments levied against your home, such as road, sewer or lighting assessments can be negotiated as well. Particularly if the assessments are being paid in installments that extend beyond the rental period to when the home is sold to the tenant-buyer. It's not uncommon for buyers to request the seller to pay the assessment in full before closing. However, you can also ask that the assessment be prorated based on when the home is sold, or even from when the rental agreement begins. I put this type of clause in my option agreement and not my rental agreement.

## Closing Cost Contributions

Usually when you do a rent-to-own, tenant-buyers do not ask for closing costs. Meaning, they do not ask for you, the seller, to pay their closing costs. Also, they may not need any help with costs or might not know they need them until they are ready to close on your home. Just be ready to update or change your documents if you decide to give them credits before closing. You can work with their lender to make this work for you both. I sometimes raise the price by the amount they need, therefore, a wash for me. I might just give them credits for their costs at closing or a portion of their costs just to make sure I get them to close on the home.

## Closing Costs

In addition to the buyer incurring closing costs at the time of sale, you as the seller, also have closing costs such as *title insurance,* and in some states *deed revenue stamps* (a.k.a. Transfer of Deed Fee). While this is not normally something that is negotiated, you can always use it as a negotiating point.

## Homeowners Association (HOA)

If you have a *Homeowners Association fee* or dues (HOA), this is something you should pay until they close on the home. If the rent is high enough to help cover this expense – great, but pay it yourself. This is an owner expense, like property taxes, and not something the average tenant would pay to rent a home or condo from someone. Remember, we want to watch out for creating *equitable interest*.

## Household Maintenance

Every home has a variety of maintenance issues. Mowing the lawn, maintaining the landscaping, snow shoveling, well and septic, pool cleaning, water softener and so on. If you have to pay for professionals to maintain all of these, the costs can really add up! Some of them, like lawn mowing and snow shoveling, the tenant-buyer can easily do themselves. This would be standard for renters. Others, like the well and septic maintenance, have to be done by a professional. You definitely want to make sure you include in your rental agreement who is responsible for all of these items or you may end up paying for them whether you wanted to or not!

## Items within the Home

Any items that will be included in the sale of the home, such as the refrigerator, stove, dishwasher, washer and dryer, a pool table, cast iron stove, etc. all have value. It's important to take that value into consideration in your negotiations. If you are including all of the appliances - the refrigerator, stove, dishwasher and washer and dryer - in your home, those items are worth thousands of dollars. Even if you had planned to include them with the house and written them off in your mind, you still want to take into account their value as you negotiate other items.

## Anything Else Between the Buyer and the Seller

You can add almost anything you want into a sales contract and can negotiate. The occupancy date, how issues from the home inspection will be handled, and so on.

As you can see, if you add up all of the different negotiation points, all of those items can be worth tens of thousands of dollars. Ignoring a little thing here or there can cost you a lot of money. Certainly, some of them you don't necessarily want to mention if the tenant-buyer doesn't bring it up, like closing cost contributions or option credits. You can always give them away at the very end, right before closing, if you need them in order to close. Some you might just include in the rental agreement as the tenant-buyer's responsibility, like household maintenance items; and then let the tenant-buyer try to negotiate them away if they don't want to pay for them.

## Wendy's Wisdom

*Remember, the goal is to SELL your home. If you over-obsess about too many negotiating points you may drive the buyers away.*

Now that we know the items we can include in our negotiations, let's take a look at some tips and tricks of HOW to negotiate in the next chapter.

# Chapter 13

## Negotiating Tips

You don't need to be an expert negotiator to negotiate successfully. It wouldn't be possible for me to teach you to be an expert negotiator in one chapter anyway. The point of this chapter is to teach you some useful tips and tricks to help you negotiate better. The reason we need to know how to negotiate is that everyone (including you) likes to negotiate to some extent.

Let me give you an example:

You have your home listed with a real estate agent for one day. You get a full price offer the first day. After the excitement of getting an offer passes, how do you feel? Bad, right? You wonder if you should have gotten more for your home or listed it higher. Now what can you do? If you accept it the exact same way it was written, you'll feel like you should have gotten more. The buyer is not going to feel good either, because they'll feel like they offered too much. Even if the offer is almost exactly what you want, you might want to change one small item – for instance ask for them to put more down, cross off that you will pay for the home warranty, something small but both you and your buyer will feel better about the deal.

When you combine these tips and tricks with the knowledge of what to negotiate that you learned in the last chapter, this will allow you to negotiate effectively for the sale of your house.

### Wendy's Wisdom

*Remember, your real estate agent can help you with negotiations. Also, most tenant-buyers will not negotiate much (except maybe the option fee).*

You will most likely, be better at negotiations than your tenant-buyers. For the most part, most tenant-buyers will not negotiate or try to negotiate much at all. Usually what I see them try to negotiate is the option fee. They might not have it all upfront and you might need to accommodate payments for them over a period of time. In other words, there is usually not much to negotiate. They want what you have and you need what they want. Most tenant-buyers are not going to go through the extent I am showing you in this chapter, but if they do, you are prepared, and if they don't you will learn ideas for other areas in your life.

**Negotiating Techniques: Keep Your Eye on the Prize**

I'm stealing this phrase from sports, but it applies here as well.

This is important for three reasons:

1.  It will keep your negotiations on track. Your main goal is to get your home sold. As you keep that in mind while you negotiate it will help you ensure that you negotiate towards that goal.

2.  By remembering what your ultimate goal is, you need to stop yourself from negotiating the deal to death. If your tenant-buyers are only doing light negotiations and you pull out the horse blankets to haggle over every little itty-bitty detail, you'll kill the deal. They will run, and run fast!

3.  If negotiations are intense and you start getting stuck on really small points, you'll lose out on the big picture. You want to sell your home. In the end it really doesn't matter too much if you concede a couple of small points, if you still achieve your end goal.

While I strongly recommend keeping your eye on your main goal, I don't recommend that you let your tenant-buyers walk all over you in the negotiations. It's okay to concede a few little sticking points if it will get the deal done. If you give in to everything just to get your home sold, it will end up being a lousy deal for you. Plus, if they had an easy time with the negotiations they'll probably keep walking all over you as your tenants.

**Remember your Goal:
Get your home SOLD!**

### Ask Questions

You want to do this both before and during negotiations. The purpose is to understand what the tenant-buyer's core motivation is. Why arc they buying a house? Once you understand what that motivation is, you can tailor your negotiations towards meeting that need. If you can meet their core motivation, for example, their apartment lease ends in two weeks and they want to be in a home before that, you'll find that it is much easier to negotiate on other points that are important to you if they can move in the home within two weeks.

When you ask questions, practice *silence after you ask*. Let them talk and listen for clues. You will learn a lot more if you zip it and let them talk.

They typically won't tell you their core need right out of the gate. By listening you can start to get some ideas, and then ask a more specific question and use silence again. It typically takes three similar questions before they'll give you their core need. For example, you might start with the question, "So why are you looking for a home

now?" In their answer they might mention that they are currently living in an apartment, so you could ask "You mentioned you are living in an apartment, what is the main reason you want a home?" In their reply they may mention that their lease will be expiring soon, so you can ask, "So with your lease ending soon you are probably looking to get into a place before that happens?"

You want to ask them open-ended questions to give them room to talk and give you details. Try not to ask a question with a yes or no answer. You can learn a lot by their answers.

### Don't Give Away Anything without Asking for Something in Return

This tit-for-tat technique helps ensure that even if you are giving your tenant-buyers a key aspect that they want, you are getting something in return. A good way to handle this is either with a question, "If I give you the $5,000 in option credits you are asking for, what do you think is a fair exchange for that?"

Or, you can ask for what you want, "If I give you the $5,000 in option credits you are asking for, I would need for you to agree to a price increase of $1,000, plus be responsible for any repairs that are necessary during the lease."

By asking a question, you give the tenant-buyer a chance to voice what they think is a fair exchange for what they are asking for. It may turn out to be MORE than what you would have asked for. If it isn't enough you can always negotiate up from what they propose.

By stating what you want, you are more limited. The tenant-buyer may even try to negotiate you down from that position. However, if there are a few key things that you really want out of the negotiation, this is a good time to go after them.

### Make Your Concessions Progressively Smaller

A lot of people make the mistake of keeping their concessions, even over the course of the negotiation. What you really want to do is to concede smaller and smaller amounts each time. Let me give you an example to illustrate what I mean.

Suppose you are asking $150,000 for your home. Your tenant-buyers offer you $140,000. You counter back at $145,000, then they counter at $142,500. So you counter at $143,750. Each time you are coming down by half.

What if you did this instead? The tenant-buyers offer you $140,000 initially and after talking with them for a while, focusing on how the home will be a benefit to them, you grudgingly come down to $148,000. They counter back at $145,000. You complain a little bit but recognize their need for a better price so you come down to $147,000. They counter back at $146,000. You say, "We're getting close. I can accept your offer at $146,500." Do you see how in the second example each counter was for progressively less money? In both examples you countered back three times. However, the end result of the first example was $143,750 and the second was $146,500; a difference of about $3,000. Three grand may not sound like a whole lot when you are talking about a $150,000 home, but think, instead of what an extra $3,000 could buy you when you get your closing check.

*Just a an idea on how to spend your extra $3,000.* ☺

## Silence is Golden -- Gets the Gold

This is one of my favorites, but the hardest for me to personally do. You can use it either after a tenant-buyer makes an offer on a negotiating point, or after you ask a question about their offer. Once you choose silence, just wait until the tenant-buyer responds. Don't be the first one to break the silence.

People aren't comfortable with silence. The longer it drags out, the more uncomfortable they'll get. Once they say something, it will be fairly likely that their position won't be as strong. I am not sure why this works, but I assume most people are like me and they feel they like they need to say something when there is silence. If they make an offer and you just stare back at them, they'll begin to think that their offer wasn't very realistic. When they break the silence, they may revise their offer upward. Even if they don't revise it up right away, they will likely be more amenable to your progressively smaller counter offers.

If you respond to their offer with a question and then silence, for example, "You are offering $140,000 for my house?", they will likely revise that amount upwards before you even have to counter their offer. For example, they might blurt out, "Well, we could go to $142,500."

## Handling Road Blocks

Sometimes negotiations get stuck. You hit a point with your tenant-buyer that neither of you are willing to concede. Usually this happens when you have both lost perspective. In other words, it becomes more important to win on that one point than to achieve your overall goal, which in your case is to sell the home. This will be rare in a rent-to-own situation, but might not be in other negotiations you do in your life.

## Wendy's Wisdom

*Just a reminder again that most tenant-buyers will not try to negotiate much. I just want you to be prepared in the event that you do need to negotiate.*

If you get stuck in your negotiations there are several things you can do to keep things moving along:

- *Try a fresh approach.* Either change your scenery (go out with your tenant-buyer for a cup of coffee and continue talking there) or try to look at the issue from a new angle. Basically, you want to try to give your mind a fresh perspective on the issue.

- *Move on to something else.* It can help to table the point you are stuck on and continue to other things. Once you have worked out other details you may not find that point to be such a stickler later.

- *Use a conditional concession.* Try the question, "If I could do this X, would you do this Y?" In this case you are saying that you are willing to give up a concession if your tenant-buyer is willing to give on something. But by phrasing it in the form of a question, you are indicating that you won't give it up without the tenant-buyer giving on something as well.

### Wince

In fact, a large portion of negotiations is non-verbal communication. Body language plays a big part by sending signals. They can range from subtle nods of the head, to the closed mind of arms being crossed. The wince is one of the most effective forms of body language. A well-used wince following an offer from tenant-buyers can convey volumes of information without having to say anything.

161

It indicates that their offer is not acceptable, and, not only is it not acceptable, it is almost painfully not acceptable.

A wince followed by stony silence can be very effective at getting the tenant-buyers to up the ante without you having to say a word.

You can also follow the wince with a question, "Is that the best you can do?"

Either way, the intent is to get the tenant-buyer to either revise their offer upward or at least mentally plant the thought that their offer is too low.

**Your Goal** → SOLD

**Remember your Goal: Get your home SOLD!**

### *Location of Negotiation*

Whenever possible you want to be the one selecting the location for your negotiations. If there is a room in your home or feature that you know the tenant-buyers fell in love with, hold the negotiations there. That will constantly reaffirm to the tenant-buyers that they want your home, and help make them more flexible as you negotiate. Otherwise you should select a room where you feel comfortable and confident, but not too relaxed. You want to feel like you have control, but not be so relaxed that you lose your edge.

### *If You Don't Ask – You'll Never Get It*

This is a pretty simple rule. If there is something you want in the negotiations, you'll never get it if you don't ask for it. You may not get it if you DO ask for it, or may only get part of it (whatever IT is, like the eBay commercials), but you must ask to have any chance of getting it. Remember, the worst they can say is "no". The answer is always "no" if you don't ask.

### The Take-Away

If negotiations are not going the way you need them to, you can consider the take-away. This is especially effective if you know the other party wants your home, or if you think they might be a real "pain" later if you don't put your foot down now.

My husband is a great salesman and he uses this often. When there are too many conditions or issues on the other side he does the take-away. When he is talking to someone and I hear him say, "You know, maybe this is not for you. Why don't we cancel your order?" or in your situation he might say, "You know I don't think my house is right for you. Maybe you should consider that other one down the street."

This might be a dangerous move because it can backfire, but many times it stops the negotiations. I can't tell you how many times the other party says to him, "No, I really do want this. I don't want to cancel." For the most part, people don't like to lose something they have become emotionally attached to.

### Don't Get Desperate

The real estate market is tough throughout much of the country right now. I know you have probably been having trouble selling your home, which is why you are going the rent-to-own option now. However, if you start to feel desperate you will start making bad decisions and give away WAY too much. If you are desperate – try to keep it to yourself (don't even share it completely with your real estate agent either).

You definitely don't want to let on to the tenant-buyer that you need to sell your home urgently. That's the same as asking them to take shameless advantage of you.

163

Here is a good point to keep in mind if you start feeling desperate: If it starts to look like the deal is falling apart, instead of giving away a bunch of concessions to save it, focus on reiterating to the tenant-buyer how their needs are being met. If you asked questions and listened earlier, you should have a good idea of what your tenant-buyer's core needs are and you'll want to bring those back up.

## Ways to Counter

Tenant-buyers also have negotiating tricks they may try to use on you. Most don't, but some might especially if you are selling a higher-end home. If you are prepared ahead of time for these, you'll have little problem responding to them if they come up during the negotiations.

### *Last Minute Add On*

This trick is used to try to capture small concessions at the last minute after everything else has been agreed upon. The idea is that once you are already emotionally invested in the deal, you don't want to let it go over just a couple of little things thrown in at the last minute.

There are a couple of effective ways to counter this technique:

- *Say no.* At this point the tenant-buyer is likely just as emotionally invested in the deal as you are, and isn't going to walk away from it if you won't give in on these last minute requests. Hopefully, you also have everything in writing, signed and the deposit in hand.

- *Counter by asking for something in return.* This is the tit-for-tat technique will allow you to meet their last minute request if they are willing to give up something in return.

This type of situation is more likely to occur with questions or requests after everything is signed. For instance, "Can we put our stuff in the garage a week early?", "Can we move in on the 28th versus the 1st since it is a weekend?", or "Can we start to paint the master bedroom before we move in?" I will usually try to accommodate these requests if I can, especially if it doesn't affect me either way. I will usually let them move in or get in early if possible. In this case I might give them free rent for those days, but they must have paid their entire balance in full to move in. I then request they also put the utilities into their name on the day they want to move in. Sometimes I even suggest this approach after we have agreed on everything. I do this so I can then reduce my expenses of utilities for a few days. Of course, all of the paperwork would be signed, as well.

### Too Many Little Things

Sometimes tenant-buyers will negotiate by progressively asking for more and more little things. Too many little things can add up to a whole lot of concessions on your part.

The most effective way to counter this is to make sure you have their entire offer before you start negotiating at all. If you have already entered into negotiations and they start throwing in more little things, stop negotiating and ask for their entire offer.

### The Alternative

The alternative is when the tenant-buyers mention that they have another house in mind. They want you to think that they are waffling between your house and another to help motivate you to make concessions.

In reality, that alternative may or may not exist.

This technique is most effective on sellers who are desperate. So it's important to not be desperate or act desperate even if you are. Also, the best way to handle this technique is to know your competition. Find out who else in your area is selling their home on a rent-to-own basis. Your real estate agent can help you with this by providing you with comparable listings. By being informed about the competition, when the tenant-buyer brings one up you can talk about why that property doesn't meet their needs as well as yours does.

## Questions

Tenant-buyers may use questions to try to determine what your core motivation is, too. It's a lot easier for them to negotiate with you if you give away too much information.

The best ways to handle their questions is to either answer their question with a question, ask them to repeat their question, or to explain what they mean, or you can answer a different question. The intent is to keep them talking and also not give away too much personal information.

## Silence

A tenant-buyer may try to use silence with you either after you make a counter offer or after asking you a question. If they use silence after you make a counter offer, the best way to counter it is with silence yourself. You've said your piece, just wait for them to respond.

If they use silence after asking you a question, ask them to explain what they meant. Get them talking again to prevent them from using this technique.

## The Wince... at you

The best way to handle someone wincing at you is to ignore it. If they wince, you can act like it didn't happen and continue on with what you are saying.

Another option is to respond with a question, "Well, what do you think?" or "Are you interested in my counteroffer?" Or you can even hit it straight on and say, "You didn't seem to like that, why?"

## *Shouting*

Shouting is an intimidation technique designed to put you off guard and make you feel as though you've really upset the other party. It is intended to be a power shift. If the tenant-buyer shouts in response to your counter offer, something like "You have to do better than that!" you can respond to it either with silence or by repeating what they say in the form of a question. If you chose silence, just stare at them until they explain more clearly what they mean. This will help prevent you from giving away additional concessions without really knowing what they are looking for.

If you chose to repeat what they say in the form of a question, you are asking them to explain themselves and clarify what they mean. Either way, you want them to be more specific about what they are looking for and to stop shouting.

Actually, I wouldn't sell to anyone that would shout at me because they'll probably keep shouting when they are tenants -- too much headache.

In my book, *Rent-to-Buy* (for buyers), I teach the other side of negotiation. I teach the buyers how to negotiate with you and what to ask for. So unless you run into a buyer that has read that book you probably won't have to negotiate too hard.

## Wendy's Wisdom

*Remember, most tenant-buyers won't be very strong negotiators. They typically negotiate most with the option fee and accept most everything else.*

In the next chapter we will discuss how to qualify your tenant-buyer to make sure they are the right ones for your home.

# Chapter 14

## Qualifying Tenant-Buyers

Great! You've found someone who is interested in your home. In addition to the negotiations we already covered, you will also need to *qualify* your prospective tenant-buyers to make sure that you should sell your home to them on a rent-to-own basis.

### Wendy's Wisdom

*Screening your tenant-buyers is a critical step. Get help for this, it will make your life much easier. Your real estate agent (if they handle tenants) can do this for you or if you are going to use a property manager they should do this.*

### Taking a Rental Application

This begins by having your prospective tenant-buyers fill out a *Rental Application*. It's a good idea to use a standard application or the one I provide in my course.

In addition to the rental application you should have them complete a *Verification of Employment (VOE)* and *Verification of Rent (VOR)* release. These will allow you to get information from their employer and landlord regarding your applicant. These are release forms that must be signed by the applicant. They are part of my course mentioned above. Most employers will not give out employee information without a signed release from the employee. Also with employment verification, it might be easier to have the tenant-buyer bring a copy of their last two paychecks. It can take weeks for some companies to get information to you about an employee. Landlords also are not supposed to give out any information without their tenant's authorization in writing.

Tenant-buyer screening checklist:

- ☐ Take rental application
- ☐ Get signed Verification of Employment and Verification of Rent releases
- ☐ Verify and make copies of Social Security Number and Driver's License Numbers
- ☐ Check paystubs (make copies)
- ☐ Verify license plate number on Car
- ☐ Perform background check -
    - o Take a look at their current residence
    - o Perform criminal background and sex offender check
    - o Perform tenant history check
- ☐ Financial qualification – review with mortgage broker

When taking an application ask to see the following and verify it is the same as on the application. You will also want to make photocopies if possible:

- ☐ Social Security Number
- ☐ Driver's License Number
- ☐ Two most recent pay stubs (1 minimum)
- ☐ Verify license plate number on car

## Verification

The next step to qualifying your tenant-buyer is verifying the information they supplied to you.

### *Verification of Employment (VOE)*

Start with the copies of the paystubs when you verify employment information. Do they show the most recent time periods? Does the amount shown correspond to the income level written on the application? I know that seems obvious but sometimes people ignore what is right in front of them.

## Wendy's Wisdom

*Look at the pay stubs. Do they show the right dates? Do they show the right company? Do they show the right income? Do they show the right person?*

Next, you need to verify that the tenant-buyer works for the employer. This is where the authorization to release comes in. Look up the employer's phone number on your own. Is it the same as the one written on the application? Call the employer and verify that the tenant-buyer works there. Confirm their income and how long they have been employed. Sometimes the written verification can take weeks. Get it started, but don't delay an approval for this long. You can accept them contingent upon final employment verification. Many times I just use the pay stubs to verify employment with a follow up call to confirm they are still with the company.

### Previous Address

Your prospective tenant-buyer may have been renting or they might have owned their own home. If they owned their home this is fairly easy to check via public records. In most states the *deed* or *title* is recorded at either the county or city level with an office like the County Recorder's Office, the Register of Deeds, or the Assessor's Office. Many areas (cities or towns) now allow you to do a property search on their website or you can go to the office and verify the information.

If the tenant-buyer lived in a rental you'll want to make sure you have the last two previous addresses. If they lived in an apartment complex you should be able to look up the contact information independently and verify it is the same as what is on the application. If it is a smaller rental (independent landlord) you will probably have to call the number provided on the rental application. A good way to verify their rental information is by asking incorrect information. Let me explain.

If the tenant-buyer has written on the application that they pay $1,000 a month in rent, you need to verify it. If they put a friend down for their landlord, the friend will lie for them and verify anything they said. If it is the real landlord they will correct you. Here is how it goes.

I call and say, "Hi, my name is Wendy and I am calling for a tenant history on Joe Blow. Can you help me on this? Are you his landlord?" They respond, "Yes, I am Joe's landlord." The way you know for sure if it is Joe's landlord versus his friend is to try this, "Joe says he pays you $1,100 a month for his rent, is this correct?" Joe's friend would say, "Yes, that is correct and he is a great tenant." Joe's real landlord would say, "Let me look that up, because I thought it was $1,000 per month. He told you $1,100? I am not sure why as his rent is $1,000." I might then say, "Oh yes, you are right it says $1,000 a month. Thanks." Having verified that you are actually talking to Joe's landlord you can then ask him to verify the length of time Joe has lived there, is he current on his rent, and if he would rent to Joe again. You should verify this information with the last two landlords. The reason is that the current landlord may want to be rid of them if they are bad tenants. That landlord may give you a glowing review just to get them out of their property. The previous landlord however, has nothing to gain or lose, so they shouldn't have any reason to lie.

Most tenant-buyers won't lie to you. However, there are some bad apples out there. These are the ones you want to clear out with your verifications. In my years as a seller with rent-to-own, I have seen bad apple tenants produce fake paystubs and use friends to act as employers and property managers. I have even had a prospective tenant-buyer who was just laid off show me their last pay stubs and tell me that they are ready to move now hoping I wouldn't call the employer to verify the employment.

## Wendy's Wisdom

*Most people are honest. Your verification process will help you screen out any dishonest tenants if you should have any apply. I don't want to scare you because the chances are low, but this way you are prepared.*

If a tenant-buyer lies on their application, reject their application and move on to the next one. If they lie now then they will lie later.

### Screening

One of the biggest mistakes people make when selling their home on a rent-to-own basis is not properly screening their tenant-buyers. Instead they go by emotion. "Well, I liked them. They seemed like really nice people." This was how I screened when I first started - by my gut and not by the law. This is a good way to GUARANTEE PROBLEMS. You will very likely end up selecting terrible tenant-buyers this way and you could be violating the law. As I mentioned, I'll cover Fair Housing Law in the next chapter. I cannot stress how important it is for you to do proper tenant screening.

Proper screening begins with verifying everything I talked about above. The next steps are about doing your proper due diligence.

### Background Check

Drive by the prospective tenant-buyer's current residence if it is close to you. How does it look from the outside? Are they taking good care of it? If there is something missing on their application, or you need them to sign another authorization to release, stop by their home unannounced. Think of something you need from them. Yes, you could easily call to have them complete it, but, that's not the point.

The idea behind stopping by their home unannounced is to see how the inside looks when they AREN'T expecting company. If it sounds rude to stop by unannounced, remember, these people may be living in YOUR home. You want people that are going to take good care of it. What if they said they have no pets, but when you show up the dog that is barking is a Rottweiler; you better think twice about these tenant-buyers. I don't like liars at all and certainly not living in my home. Are their kids' toys all over the lawn? Is the refrigerator on the front porch? Or does this tenant-buyer have a nicely manicured lawn, recently cut and well maintained. Is their home clean and did they invite you in with no hesitation?

*If your applicant's yard looks like this you might want to think twice!*

The rental application should also request non-related references. You should call each person listed. You aren't going to learn anything startling from these references. After all, the tenant-buyer wouldn't list them if they weren't going to give a positive recommendation. The reason to call them is because the references will tell the tenant-buyer that you called. This helps the tenant-buyer know that you are doing proper checking. It also gives you real references if anything goes wrong later and you need to track the tenant-buyers down.

### Criminal Background Check

By and large it's a pretty good idea not to let people that are convicted felons move into your home. Then again, many people feel the same way about IRS auditors or attorneys, so you'll have to make the decision for yourself. Either way, if you decide to do a criminal check as part of your process to screen your application, you will need to do it on everyone; not just the ones that look like felons. Many states now offer the ability to do this via the internet. I've found the best way to do a background search is by starting with the state government website and then going to the law enforcement section. You may find a link for doing criminal record searches there. Many states will charge for this type of search. For example:

- In the State of Michigan the web address is (no www in front) – apps.michigan.gov/ichat/home.aspx

- In the State of Florida it's - www.fdle.state.fl.us/criminalhistory

- In the State of Washington it's (no www in front) - watch.wsp.wa.gov

There are also MANY commercial websites that claim to search criminal records throughout the US. Since I use the state law enforcement agency sites, I can't attest to the accuracy or quality of any of those sites. If you want to try one of them, just do a web search for criminal record check or criminal background check.

### Sex Offender Registry

In addition to the criminal background check there is also a great FREE website called Family Watchdog: www.familywatchdog.us/default.asp.

This allows you to search for convicted sex offenders by name or by location. Understand these sites may not be 100% accurate so don't judge everything on the results from this site. Dig deeper if you find something you want to verify on this site. If you find something on this site, ask the applicant directly to deny or confirm what you found.

### *Tenant History Check*

There are also websites available that will help you screen your prospective tenant-buyer for tenant history. They can check for evictions and outstanding financial judgments. The quality of these sites tends to vary, often based on the population of the area. In other words, rural areas may not have as strong quality data as metropolitan areas. Additionally, evictions and other civil judgments are not recorded by social security number; they are only recorded by name. This means that if your tenant-buyer has a unique name like Vladimir Braithwaite, you will be more successful in your search than if you tenant-buyer has a name like Jill Smith.

Even with the limitations, the sites can still be quite useful. There are some sites I have used with good results. To get current information on sites I recommend, check out my website and go to the Rent-to-Own site. All the tools to sell your home will be under the *SELL Your Home* link.

### *Credit Reports*

Another critical component in evaluating your prospective tenant-buyer is their credit. After all, they will need to get a mortgage down the road when they buy your home. We know before we pull their credit that for most of them, they will not be stellar reports. If they were, they might not need to buy a rent-to-own.

Credit reports can be tricky to navigate and difficult to understand. Fortunately, there is no need for you to do so. Instead of trying to interpret credit reports on your own, enlist the assistance of a mortgage broker to do it for you. If you don't know of a good mortgage broker, check my website for one that works nationwide. They can usually run a credit report for you at no charge. They will want the mortgage business when the tenant-buyer buys the home from you.

## Wendy's Wisdom

*There is no need for you to understand the intricacies of credit reports. Enlist the help of a mortgage broker.*

Have your tenant-buyer applicant meet with the mortgage broker so the broker can pull their credit and analyze it for you. Working with a mortgage broker that understands rent-to-own transactions will be a big benefit. We will talk later in Chapter 18 about having your tenant-buyer stay in touch with the mortgage broker or vice-versa to stay on track with repairing their credit.

Once the mortgage broker has given you their analysis you'll find that there are 4 types of buyers when it comes to credit:

1. *Good credit* - this type of buyer doesn't usually have to do a rent-to-own. They can usually qualify for a mortgage, however, they may be sitting on the fence when it comes to buying and want to wait and see what happens with the market. They might also have another home that hasn't sold yet. We are  starting to see more and more with the mortgage industry changes. Sellers cannot get another mortgage in some cases until they sell their home.

2. *Bad credit with no excuse* - this type of buyer has lousy credit but no reason for it. They make enough money, but are just lazy about paying their bills on time (or paying them at all). They have the money managing sense of Bear Stearns. This is not the type of buyer you want in your home. Can you say DEADBEAT?

3. *Bad credit with a reason* - this type of tenant-buyer had something happen to them that caused their credit to plunge. Whether it is job loss, divorce, medical problem or even that the interest rate on  their old mortgage increased too high for them to be able to make the payment, something happened that damaged their credit. You'll need to determine with the assistance of a mortgage broker if they are still heading down a bad path or if they are working their way back up with their credit.

4. *Unknown* - this type of tenant-buyer has bad credit but it is too recent or too hard to tell if they are working to improve. This type of person will turn into either a #2 buyer or a #3 buyer, which means they are  either just a lazy deadbeat that you don't want in your house, or they will work to improve their credit. It can be difficult to determine which. If your mortgage broker is unable to give you a clear determination, you might be better off passing. I do have one exception to this rule: if the tenant-buyer has a lot down for their option fee (i.e. 5-10% versus 1-2%) then I might accept them.

When it comes to the best type of applicant to get, the tenant-buyer who works to rebuild their credit is the one MOST likely to close on the sale down the road. This is not to say that other types won't, but they are your best bet. They will be the most grateful to you for giving them the chance to get their next home.

## Property Management Companies

If all of the above screening sounds like too much work for you, there are property management companies that can handle both the initial screening as well as manage your home for you while the tenant-buyer is renting.

## Wendy's Wisdom

*I recommend using a property manager if you can afford one. If you live far away from your rent-to-own home it's almost essential.*

Property management companies can take a lot of the headache out of being a landlord. Reading all of this might be enough to give you a headache!

They will screen your prospective tenant-buyers for you and give you an analysis. Then, once you have selected a tenant-buyer, they will handle the rent collection as well as any issues that arise during the rental period.

There are a few caveats to property management, however. First, of course, is they want to be paid for their work. In addition to the initial tenant placement fee you will also have to pay a monthly management fee.

Second, not all property managers are created equal. If you do choose to use property management for your home you will want to select your property manager with some care to make sure that your interests will be well represented. Do you need a recommendation on a property manager in your area? Email me at refer@wendypatton.com. Many times a property manager can be your real estate agent, too.

## The Numbers

Another important aspect to take into consideration when choosing your tenant-buyer is whether or not they can afford your home.

As a general rule of thumb you would want their gross monthly income to be equal to three times the monthly rental rate. However, you do want to take into account their other financial obligations. This is where a mortgage broker can assist you with the numbers. Although rental rates can be lower than their mortgage payment when they buy, I still qualify my tenant-buyer on the rental rate.

If the rental rate for your home is $1,200 per month, following the general rule you would want your tenant-buyer to be grossing $3,600+ per month. If they also have a lot of other debts, like two car payments for $400 and $450 per month, plus credit card payments of $400 per month and a medical judgment with monthly payments of $250 per month, you can quickly add up the numbers to see they won't have any money left for utilities or groceries. Guess who won't get paid? YOU!

## Wendy's Wisdom

*If there is a big difference between what your home will rent for versus what the buyer's end mortgage payment will be, take a look at this next example.*

## How to Get More Rent for Your Home

If you live in an area like California, many $500,000 homes rent for $2,500 per month. This rental amount will leave the tenant-buyer far from paying the estimated $3,500-$4,500 they will have to pay when they get a mortgage.

Keep this in mind as it can "de-motivate" your tenant-buyer from closing. Who would want to pay an extra $1,000 - $2,000 per month to own versus rent? Here is an idea for you to try.

You advertise the home based on market rent so you get interested tenant-buyers, but when you find someone you, offer them a special deal. I have two ideas for you:

1. You see if they can afford more based on their *rental application*. If they can you can use this idea. You ask them if they would like a 50% return on their money. They say, "Yes." You say, "Well if you are willing to pay $1,000 more per month, I will give you the $1,000 per month you are paying, plus an extra $500 per month towards buying this home." This at least gets them to $3,500 per month which is a small jump, if any, to the larger mortgage payment, and it also gets them more money built up to buy the home. They won't want to lose a large amount of money. If they choose not to buy you get to keep the extra money, but if they choose to buy they get a large credit from you. Either way it was good for you – because you got $1,000 more per month to help with your bills.

If they do agree to this choice, make the rent in the *rental agreement* $3,500 and you show the credit in the *option agreement* (*not the rental agreement*).

2. You can offer choices with your applicants. Here is the idea behind this:

   - Rent of $2,500 per month with a $15,000 option fee

   - Rent of $2,800 per month with a $12,000 option fee

   - Rent of $3,300 per month with a $5,000 option fee

You get the idea. This strategy can be used in any price range of home. I don't put it in my ad this way as it can be confusing to the reader, but I explain this at the home when I find out if they are interested.

With all of this said, a mortgage broker will help you with this analysis. Use professionals to help you with all of this, so it is not difficult or overwhelming.

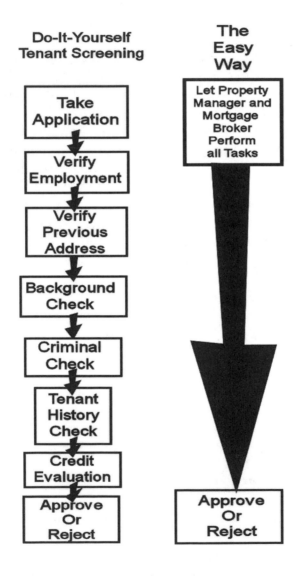

*It is up to you whichever one you like the best.*

Remember, your goal is not to do everything yourself, but to sell your home.

Once you have completed all of the screening, you need to decide yea or nay. If they aren't the right tenant-buyer for you, you will need to reject their application and move on to the next prospective tenant-buyer. If they are the right one, you can move on to Chapter 16 where we will go over the checklist before they move in. Do the screening and selection or rejection quickly. You do NOT want them to go somewhere else before you decide if you want them. Use the *Non-Refundable Deposit* form now, if you haven't already gotten a deposit from them.

## Wendy's Wisdom

*Approve or deny the applicant quickly - 1-3 days – or communicate with them if longer.*

In the next chapter we will cover the Federal Law on Fair Housing. These are things you want to take very seriously so you will definitely want to read this chapter.

# Chapter 15

# Fair Housing Law

U.S. Department of Housing and Urban Development:

> "Title VIII of the Civil Rights Act of 1968 (Fair Housing Act), as amended, prohibits discrimination in the sale, rental, and financing of dwellings, and in other housing-related transactions, based on race, color, national origin, religion, sex, familial status (including children under the age of 18 living with parents of legal custodians, pregnant women, and people securing custody of children under the age of 18), and handicap (disability)."

**What this Means**

*Fair Housing Law* really isn't that complicated. In a nutshell, this means you cannot discriminate against any protected class. When it comes to selling or renting your home, by law, you cannot discriminate against anyone based on their:

- Race or color: meaning the color of their skin or their cultural race

- National origin: meaning the country they are from

- Religion: whether they are Christian, Muslim, Buddhist, atheist or any other religion

- Sex: male or female

- Familial status: whether they have children or not

- Disability: whether they are disabled – physically or mentally

And honestly, why would you want to? Get a qualified person in your home! That is your goal! There are also other categories that are protected in many states:

- Marital status: whether the tenant-buyers are married or not

- Age: how old they are

- Sexual Orientation: heterosexual, bisexual, homosexual, asexual.

Many states and some municipalities have additional protected classes. So you will need to be aware of those if you are thinking about excluding anyone. Although, to date, I'm pretty sure that you can still exclude lawyers anywhere in the country (just kidding lawyers, but you really can).

Seriously, you can exclude a profession or a smoker. These areas are not protected by Fair Housing Laws. I can't imagine too many professions you would exclude, however a drug dealer might be one and so might a lion tamer (remember one of those guys in Vegas almost didn't make it). Plus the lion might be in violation if you have a "no pet" policy.

An additional class that is protected by different law is source of income. This particularly applies to Section 8 housing. A landlord cannot prohibit someone from renting based on the fact that they receive Section 8 housing assistance in *some* states.

However, in a rent-to-own situation this would probably not apply because they wouldn't be able to afford to purchase your home down the road and would fail tenant screening when meeting with a mortgage broker.

If you want to know what additional classes are protected in your state, www.Craigslist.org has most of them posted (this is not guaranteed to be complete for your area and does not cover municipalities): http://www.Craigslist.org/about/FHA#categories

## Wendy's Wisdom

*As a reminder after reading all of that - it's very easy to stay in compliance with whatever laws might exist in your area – just don't discriminate. Judge and qualify an applicant based on their application only.*

### Set Your Standards in Writing

It's a very good idea to take a few minutes to have your tenant-buyer acceptance standards in writing. This gives you legal protection should any disputes arise. These written guidelines would define the terms under which a tenant-buyer can be rejected. For example, if they have been evicted from another residence, they would not qualify.

You must enforce these standards equally to all prospective applicants. These standards cannot allow you to discriminate against any protected class.

Here are my standards so you can see what I mean. Notice I am not restricted, because I need to apply this to any and all applications and accept the FIRST qualified applicant. I don't put credit score on my list, because credit scores can be very low right after a bankruptcy or foreclosure, but yet the person might be a great candidate for a rent-to-own.

1. No landlord/tenant judgments unpaid

2. Ability to pay outstanding judgments/collections

3. Good landlord reference (prefer two references)
4. Verified income to qualify for 3-4x rent

5. If bankruptcy, must be discharged

6. Option fee available or negotiated

7. Prefer they have spoken to a mortgage representative

These standards are pretty lenient. If you prefer, you can make yours more restrictive. For example, you'll notice I don't have anything about criminal convictions – you may choose to have a standard that says no felony convictions.

Let's say you reject someone's rental application for example, because they only make 2 ½ times the rental rate in income and they accuse you of discrimination. You can then show your written guidelines that clearly indicate that applicants must have verified income 3 to 4 times higher than the rental amount to qualify. After all, if they can't afford the rent, they won't be able to afford a mortgage. If you deny someone to live in your home you should send a letter with the reason. There is an example letter in my course materials.

**Common Mistakes**

*Selecting a Tenant-Buyer that Will Make Your Neighbors Happy*

Hey, you are moving on, who cares about the neighbors anymore! Just kidding, of course you care about them and are probably very good friends with some of them. You certainly don't want to place a deadbeat near your friends for their sake or yours. Most of us like our neighbors and want to keep them happy with the next person moving into our home. Unless of course you have lousy neighbors (which is why you moved) and you want to be vindictive by letting a weirdo move into your home.

However, if you try to keep your neighbors happy by making sure the tenant-buyers that are moving into your home are like your neighbors - for example, the same skin color, religion or any other protected class you are guilty of violating Fair Housing Law. Off to jail with you; do not pass go, do not collect $200. Okay, I am not sure there is a jail sentence, but the fine for Fair Housing violations for your first offense can be up to $11,000 in civil penalties PLUS the discriminated party can sue you for damages and those penalties can be MUCH higher. I doubt you want to mess with this. If you have that much money to mess around with, just drop the price of your home and move on.

Just as a side note, Fair Housing Law applies to either the sale or rental of your home. So even if you were selling conventionally you would still have to follow the law.

### A Few Common Advertising Mistakes

If you make your own flyers and post your own ads in the paper or the internet, it's easy to violate Fair Housing Law. Usually it is from putting something on the ad about who the home is good for or what you are looking for in tenant-buyers. Just stick to the details about the house and the terms and you'll be fine. Here are a couple of advertising examples that are BIG NO-NOs:

- "Home is perfect for young couple looking for their first home" –violates age and possibly marital status

- "Wanted: a good Christian family" – violates religion and familial status
- "Smaller home, good for single person or couple with no children" – violates familial and marital status

- "Mostly Hispanic neighborhood" – violates race/color

Do not advertise like this and do not ask questions about their family, kids, or anything like that when they call you or meet you in person. You can ask, "How many people will be living in the home," but not, "How many children do you have?" This is the one I hear violated the most.

## *Rental Application Mistakes*

- Asking questions about a person's disability

- Asking if a (disabled) person is able to live independently

- Asking whether the applicant and co-applicant are married

- Asking them to name their children

- Requiring proof of U.S. citizenship as part of the application. This one is a bit tricky. While you can't discriminate based on national origin, some states now have laws that will penalize you, the landlord, if you rent to an illegal alien. As part of your documentation purposes you may ask to see proof of citizenship or a green card, or a State Department issued Visa that permits them to legally be in the United States.

## *Changing the Terms of the Deal to Keep Someone Out*

If you try to change the terms, like increase the rent or the purchase price or the option fee, because the prospective tenant-buyer is a different ethnic background from you or is in a wheelchair, or any other discriminating reason, you're going to "the bad place" (think fire and brimstone). Well, maybe or maybe not, but after HUD has done their fair housing enforcement on you, it will feel like you have been there and back. Plus you'll be broke because the fines for violation are hefty.

Also, if you try to change the terms of the deal *in favor of someone*, for example, John Smith goes to your church so you'll cut him a better deal, then you are just as guilty. Even if God won't punish you because he goes to your church, the U.S. government will. Now with this said, if no one else applies, you can reduce your standards and accept your friend from church or anywhere for that matter.

### *No-Pet Policy*

If you have a No-Pet policy for your prospective tenant-buyers you MUST make an exception for a handicapped person with a guide dog. Additionally, if you have a no-pet policy and receive an application from a handicapped person, you cannot suddenly institute a pet deposit or monthly pet fee.

### *Reasonable Accommodation*

If a disabled person applies for your home and asks you to add an entrance ramp to the home and modify the bathroom so it is handicap accessible you cannot deny them this right. You must allow reasonable accommodation. However, the changes made to your home, such as the ramp, would be at their expense, not yours.

Additionally, if they elect to not purchase your home, they must return the home to its original condition. As a security measure for yourself, you might ask to have the funds to restore the home escrowed to ensure that it will happen. However, you should talk with an attorney before requiring the escrow, to make sure that's legal. Remember, if you sign up for Pre-Paid Legal you can ask this question of an attorney at no additional charge to you.

### *Linguistic Profiling*

If you don't bother to return phone calls inquiring about your rent-to-own home from a prospective tenant-buyer because from the sound of their voice you think they are black or an immigrant, but do return phone calls from other people you could be in deep doo-doo.

### *Neighborhood Makeup*

If you are showing an Asian prospective tenant-buyer the home and tell them, "Oh, you'll like the neighborhood. Most everyone here is also Asian." You'd better call an attorney. I wouldn't recommend calling an attorney that you've excluded either, because they won't give you very good representation.

If you tell a prospective tenant-buyer the racial makeup of your neighborhood - EVEN if they are of the same race - you are in violation. It doesn't matter if they are the same race or not. If they ask, you should tell them to check out public records if they want to know the make-up of the neighborhood. You can be friendly about it and say that even if you did know the details, you would not be able to share them because of Fair Housing Laws.

## Wendy's Wisdom

*When it comes to Fair Housing Law what I don't recommend is this: pretending that it doesn't exist.*

I think I made my point. I am sure most of you would never do any of these violations on purpose, however you might do them with good intentions or by accident. The main point – TREAT EVERYONE THE SAME! There is no reason not to. You want the best qualified tenant-buyer.

The law states that you must accept the **first qualified tenant** that applies.

In the next chapter we'll focus on what to do after you've approved your prospective tenant-buyer. Now it get's exciting because you have found someone to buy your home. It's time to get them in it so you can move on.

# Chapter 16

## Approved! – What do I do Next?

Once you have approved your tenant-buyer you have a few little details to take care of, you know, things like moving out of your house (if you haven't already), signing contracts and so forth.

I have provided you with a checklist in this chapter that covers all of these details.

This makes it very easy for you. As long as you check each thing off on the list, it will keep you on track.

If something doesn't apply to your situation, you can just check it off before you start.

Let's take a look at the list, then go into detail on each item.

## *Rent-to-Sell Checklist*

- ☐ Advertise your home
- ☐ Get Application Fee with Filled-out Rental Application
- ☐ Get Non-Refundable Deposit.
- ☐ Confirm Applicant Meets Criteria:
    - ○ Verification of Employment (VOE)
    - ○ Verification of Rent (VOR)
- ☐ If not approved, send letter of denial to applicant
- ☐ Create Folder for all documents pertaining to your home sale
- ☐ Draft Rental Agreement/Option Agreement/Sales Contract
- ☐ Change your Homeowner's Insurance to Rental Insurance
- ☐ Videotape home (with tenant if possible) or get pictures of entire home (put in folder with other papers)
- ☐ Get Check-In/Out List to tenant-buyer
- ☐ Cancel any home sale advertising
- ☐ Sign Rental Agreement, Option Agreement, Sales Contract & Pet Agreement
- ☐ Sign Lead Based Paint & Sellers Disclosure
- ☐ Collect additional deposit
- ☐ Confirm that the tenant-buyer transferred utilities to their name
- ☐ Transfer gas, electric, garbage, water, water softener, etc. to tenant-buyer's name
- ☐ Confirm the tenant-buyer has returned the Check-In/Out List
- ☐ Confirm the tenant-buyer has Renter's Insurance
- ☐ Remove any sign(s) and any lockbox (if applicable)
- ☐ Make a copy of tenant-buyer's personal checks – put in the folder every month
- ☐ Confirm the tenant-buyer is working with a mortgage lender and/or a credit repair company - continue to follow up

Let's go over these step by step. Note that they might not be in the exact order for your situation. Some steps may all happen the same day, or one before another due to your particular situation. (note: all checklists in this book can be downloaded at www.WendyPatton.com/checklists)

## *Advertise Your Home*

We went into details on this in Chapter 7. Do everything you can to get the word out that you are selling your home as a rent-to-own.

## *Get Application Fee with Filled out Rental Application*

Once the tenant-buyers decide they want your home they need to fill out a rental application. You will use this application as the basis for screening your prospective tenant-buyer.

*Blaring loudspeakers 24 hours a day might be too much!*

Also, if you are charging an application fee (to cover the costs associated with tenant screening) you would collect it at this time. Typically this would be in the range of $25 to $40 per applicant. I charge this to everyone in the home over the age of 18.

## *Get Non-Refundable Deposit (with signed deposit form)*

You may take a deposit from the tenant-buyers at the time they submit their application or, once you have approved them. This secures the unit for them so you won't sell or rent it to someone else. If, for some reason, they change their mind, they lose the deposit; so make sure it is enough to protect you. This deposit is NOT the option fee, but it will later become part of the option fee

195

when they sign the documents. The deposit will apply towards their total move-in cost such as first month's rent and the option fee. You will want to get as much as you can from the tenant-buyer in the form of a check or cash, but also understand some people might only have $100 or $200 on them. You can ask for more to add to this as soon as you approve them. I recommend you get as much as possible to prevent them from changing their minds. If you collect any deposit before you approve their application, this would be refundable if their application is denied. The only money you keep is the application fee if you choose to reject them.

This form also acknowledges that you received this deposit and that they acknowledge that the deposit is non-refundable.

### Confirm Applicant Meets Criteria

We covered this in Chapter 14. If you do the proper screening you will make your life much easier. Remember to use your tenant qualifications list and obey all of the rules of Fair Housing Law.

If you reject a tenant-buyer's application you must notify them in writing. You can tell them verbally if you choose, but, by law, you must also provide them with the written rejection. State clearly why they were not approved based on your requirement criteria. There is no need to beat around the bush, be straightforward and honest. Don't be rude or brutal, though.

### Create Folder to Put All Documents in for Your Home Sale

Organization is important. Creating a folder to put all items regarding the sale of your rent-to-own home in will save you a lot of time and frustration. Any time you have something regarding the sale of your home put it into this folder, including copies of the checks you receive from your tenant-buyer each month.

> *"Organizing is what you do before you do something, so that when you do it, it is not all mixed up." – A. A. Milne, creator of Winnie-the-Pooh.*

### *Draft Rental Agreement/Option Agreement/Sales Contract*

You want to prepare the contracts before the tenant-buyer moves in. This way you have everything ready to go. I go into detail on this in my course with an audio step-by-step instruction CD to assist you.

Remember, as we talked about in Part 3, not all contracts are created equal. If the tenant-buyer or the tenant-buyer's real estate agent offers to prepare the contracts you will be getting neutral contracts at best. At worst you may be stuck with contracts that favor the buyer instead of you.

Protect yourself with good contracts. You can do this by putting in extra clauses that are *pro-seller*.

### *Change Your Homeowner's Insurance to Rental Insurance*

Since you will no longer be living in the home, it is no longer necessary to cover the contents; your possessions. You just need to insure the dwelling. Call your insurance company and tell them that you will be turning your home into a rental and need to change the insurance policy. Talk to them about lost rent if something were to happen to your home and you couldn't rent it for a period of time – this will help cover your mortgage payment. Decide with them what coverage you will want to take out on your home now that it is a rental home.

You may also want to shop around for better rates and/or better coverage as a rental. Typically rental insurance is either about the same cost or it can be a little less than homeowner's insurance.

### *Video Tape Home (with tenant if possible) or Get Pictures of Entire Home (put in folder with other papers)*

197

It's very important to have some method of documenting the condition of your home at the time the tenant-buyer takes possession. The common method is to have a unit condition form (check in/out form) where the tenant walks through the home room by room and marks any damages or defects on the form. Another method is to walk through the home with your tenant-buyer, videotaping the entire home, with the tenant-buyer in the video when you are taping it. Do both if you can and get it in writing if you can only do one.

When you do the video recording it's important to have the date of the recording showing on the screen. Also ask the tenant-buyer questions, such as "How do the kitchen cabinets look to you?" or "Do you see any issues in the living room?" These questions establish that the tenant-buyer was with you and acknowledged the condition of your home. You can also ask them to verify the date. This is just extra protection for you.

The whole reason for doing this is such that if the tenant-buyer doesn't purchase your home you have documented evidence of the condition if you deduct any money for damages from the security deposit. If the tenant-buyer tries to contest the condition you have proof with them in the video. In writing is always better for the court, but a video is not bad additional protection.

## Wendy's Wisdom

*Videotaping the condition of your home can be handy, but remember, if you can only do one thing make to get the condition of the home in writing.*

### Get Check-In/Out List to Tenant-Buyer

This is the property condition form that they sign off on the condition of your home. This protects you and them if they don't buy, and you need to prove the condition of the home. In other words, if damage was done to the home and they didn't purchase it, you now have proof of what the condition was when they moved in. I recommend they also sign and date it for you. You might want to walk through the home and do it together so you have it in your records right away. Make them a copy for their files too.

### *Cancel Any Advertising*

You don't want to take your home off the market until the tenant-buyer has signed all of the paperwork and handed over the money. However, any advertising that you are paying for you may want to cancel once you receive the non-refundable deposit. The reason for this is that should the deal fall through somehow, you are still marketing your home to find another tenant-buyer.

### *Sign Rental Agreement, Option Agreement, Sales Contract & Pet Agreement*

You will both need to sign the sales contract, rental agreement, and option agreement. If possible you want to sign these in advance, before move-in day. The sooner the better for you because it prevents the tenant-buyer from changing his or her mind and backing out. Bring a pen or two!

### *Sign Lead Based Paint & Seller's Disclosure*

This disclosure is required by federal law. Even if your home was built after 1978, you still need to complete one. You are also required to provide the pamphlet "Protect your family from lead in your home."

You can ask your real estate agent about how to get one or print one from the following link: http://www.cpsc.gov/cpscpub/pubs/426.pdf. Your real estate agent should make sure this happens for you and will have the appropriate forms.

A seller's disclosure is a statement of the condition of your home. As discussed earlier, it is the law in most states that you provide this and disclose anything wrong with your home. If you know your basement leaked, even if it is now fixed, you will want to disclose that. It is not hard for a buyer later to prove that you knew this (neighbors remember you talking about it or having the repair truck there). These forms will likely have some variations, so you will need to get the form specific to your state. The best way to get the forms you need for your state is from your real estate agent. I have a Seller's Disclosure form in my course that is generic. Make sure it will be okay to use in your state.

## Collect Additional Deposit

It's time to start getting paid! You need to collect the first full month's rent as well as a prorated first month's rent if they are moving in mid-month. You also need to collect the option fee and possibly a security deposit. Hopefully you got much of this when they signed the Non-Refundable Deposit form, but here is where you collect the remainder of the deposit or any outstanding balance. If you only collected $300 with the Non-Refundable Deposit form, and your option fee is $5,000 the tenant-buyer would still owe $4,700 plus the first month's rent. You might want to get another Non-Refundable Deposit form signed if this is the situation and they are not moving in for a month or more. I like to get as much down and as soon as possible once the buyers are approved. I suggest you do the same thing. Remember, *no personal checks* unless they have time to clear the bank before they move into your home. If they are paying some on the move-in date, make sure it is certified funds.

Any non-refundable deposit that was made earlier should be deducted from the amount due. When you are going to meet with them to sign the paperwork, let them know how much to bring before they arrive so they can be prepared. If they are not bringing the rest of their deposit on the day they sign, then you will need to make sure you collect it prior to turning over the keys.

Sometimes they will not have the full amount by the day they sign the documents (which you still will want signed as quickly as you can) and they may owe a balance the day you turn over the keys to them. Remember though all money at this point is in certified funds, not a personal check, UNLESS it has the time to clear our bank before they move in.

The reason you want this separate is should the tenant-buyer chose not to purchase the home, the security deposit can be used for unpaid rent or damages to the home and then the balance returned to the tenant-buyer. Additionally, and probably more importantly, is that if you don't collect a security deposit and the tenant-buyer doesn't buy the house and tried to sue you to collect the option fee it may be considered a security deposit by the court. This is easily preventable by collecting a separate security deposit. It doesn't have to be large but something – for instance $200.

This is not to scare you and it is rare, but if you are the type that likes to play it safe, put a little into the security deposit spot. This is more important in "pro-tenant" areas like California, but not as important in my city. In my area I always put 100% of what they have in option fee so it is non-refundable.

**Move in Day**

It's finally here! By this time you will need to have moved out of your home so you can move on with your life. You need to leave your home clean and ready for the tenant-buyers to move in. Before you actually move out however, make sure that the tenant-buyers are moving in. As I said before, you want to try to sign the contracts before this day as a protection measure for yourself.

***Confirm that the
Tenant-Buyer
Transferred
Utilities to Their Name***

BEFORE you give possession of your home to the tenant-buyer you absolutely must make sure they have transferred all of the utilities to their name. Call the utility companies yourself to confirm. Even if you just call to confirm, you should also arrange to have the utilities taken out of your name effective the day the tenant-buyers will be moving in. That way, if there is any mistake, you will not still be stuck paying for the tenant-buyer's utilities.

I made this mistake once. The tenant promised me she would transfer the utilities and months went by before she finally got around to it. That was only after I finally told her that I was shutting them off. Guess what? I had a very hard time collecting the money for the charges for before that point. So, now I always make sure they are in their name now and I shut them off and out of my name the day they move in.

In some areas the water bill, if not paid, can become a lien on the property. If this is the case where you live, find out if you can have a copy mailed to you to see if they are being paid. If they are not you can pay yourself and bill your tenant-buyer. In that case you will want to have a clause in the lease that the tenant-buyer will receive a copy of the water bill from you and they are to pay you. Or, you send them a copy of the water bill and they pay it and send you a copy of their receipt of payment. This way you can ensure the water bill actually gets paid.

### *Confirm the Tenant-Buyer Returned the Check-In/Out List*

After the tenant-buyer has moved in, this list must be signed by the tenant-buyer and returned to you. Make sure you follow up if they haven't returned it. Once you get it from them be sure to put it in your folder. Try to get them to do it on the spot with you so you are not trying to track it down later.

### *Confirm the Tenant-Buyer has Renter's Insurance*

This is not an absolute requirement but you should document in writing that you requested they obtain renter's insurance, send follow up letters if they haven't, and keep copies of these requests. This protects you should anything happen to their possessions in your home. You have documented evidence that you encouraged them to obtain renter's insurance.

Why do they need it? If something happened to the home (fire/flood) or it was broken into, your property insurance will not cover their personal property. They have to have renter's insurance to cover personal items.

It is also a good idea to have a clause in the lease indicating that you as the homeowner will keep insurance on the dwelling but the tenant is responsible for insuring all of their possessions.

## Wendy's Wisdom

*When they get their renter's insurance have them name you as additional insured. Some insurance companies will not do this, but most will. This will give you some liability protection should something happen or someone is injured in your home.*

*You have liability insurance on your homeowner's policy, but this extra protection doesn't hurt.*

### Remove any Sign(s) and Any Lockbox (if applicable)

That's it. Your home is now officially a rent-to-own home with a tenant-buyer in place. Take any signs you have in front of the house as you leave. If the signs and the lockbox belong to your real estate agent make sure they take them out.

### Make a Copy of Tenant-Buyer's Personal Checks – Put in the Folder Every Month

Each month, when the tenant-buyer pays you, make a copy of the payment for documentation purposes. You'll want this for yourself for tax purposes and for legal protection.

### Confirm the Tenant-Buyer is Working with a Mortgage Lender and Credit Repair Company - Continue to Follow Up

Now that they are in your home make sure that they are taking the steps so they can get a mortgage and BUY your home. I'll go into more details on this in Chapter 18.

You should also give your tenant-buyer this checklist to help them stay on track during their tenancy.

### Buyer Checklist During Tenancy

☐ Home inspection completed on _____

☐ Meet with a mortgage broker and set up a plan

☐ Get into Credit Repair

☐ Always pay with a personal check or cashier's check that comes from your bank account

☐ Pay on-time monthly rent payments and in full

☐ Pay all bills on-time to clean up credit

☐ Continue to follow up with mortgage broker on credit status

All checklists in this book can be printed from www.WendyPatton.com/checklist.

Congratulations! With a tenant-buyer in place you can now move on with your life. In the next chapter we will cover how to ensure that everyone is getting paid. Making sure the tenant pays the rent and the bank receives the mortgage payment.

# PART 5

## WHAT TO DO DURING THE RENT-TO-OWN AND HOW TO CLOSE THE DEAL

# Chapter 17

## Making Sure Everyone Gets Paid

Making sure everyone is getting paid is essential to successfully selling your rent-to-own home. There are multiple components that need to be paid, such as the tenant-buyer paying you the rent, your mortgage company getting the mortgage payment, the real estate agent (if you used one) getting their commission, and of course you getting paid when you sell your home.

In some cases, both you and the tenant-buyer will want confirmation that the mortgage payment is being paid. No matter what, make sure you get that payment made each month and do not put the tenant-buyer's investment in your home in jeopardy. If they read my book _Rent-to-Buy_ (for buyers), they will definitely request proof of your payment each month. Most buyers will not even think about that situation or bring it up, but do make sure you are making those payments and not jeopardizing their rights and ability to buy your home.

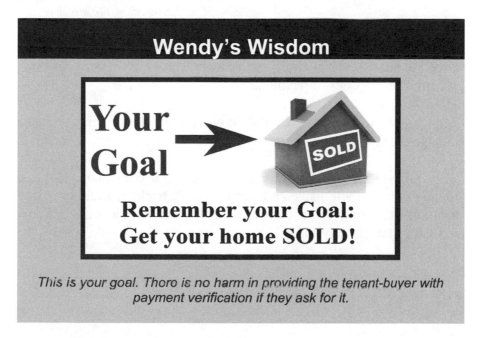

### Wendy's Wisdom

**Your Goal** → **SOLD**

**Remember your Goal:
Get your home SOLD!**

*This is your goal. There is no harm in providing the tenant-buyer with payment verification if they ask for it.*

## Paying the Rent

Obviously, getting paid by the tenant-buyer is critical for you. It doesn't matter to you so much HOW the tenant-buyer pays you so long as they actually DO pay you. Well, I suppose you probably wouldn't want to accept food stamps or homemade pies, but, when it comes time to qualify for a mortgage for the tenant-buyer, it is very important HOW they paid you. The tenant-buyer must have a documentable paper trail of payments. Their mortgage lender needs to be able to verify that the tenant-buyer's payments were made to you each month.

The best way to do this is for the tenant-buyer to pay you with a personal check, or a cashier's check from their bank account each month. This creates the documentable paper trail that most mortgage lenders need.

This is one time cash is not king!

*Sorry Ben, not this time*

Even though cash is great for you, when the tenant-buyer goes to qualify for a mortgage, the mortgage company will not accept cash as proof of payments.

Remember your goal and do what works to get your buyers a mortgage.

If your tenant-buyers come to meet you with cash, tell them to go back to their bank and put the cash back in their checking account and bring you a certified check from that account. I know it's hard to turn away cash.

## Wendy's Wisdom

*Payment methods that are NOT good for qualifying for a mortgage down the road - cash or someone else's personal check.*

Everything must be documented and have a paper trail. I won't accept a personal check before they move in, unless it has time to clear. After they are in your house a personal check is fine and preferred for mortgage companies.

However, if the tenant-buyer bounces a check you'll want to have them start paying you via bank issued checks. One bounced check should be your limit. They'll need to keep copies of the bank checks. You also should make and keep a copy of their initial option fee check and each month's payment thereafter.

## Wendy's Wisdom

*Remember to make sure you are organized! After everything is signed with the tenant-buyer keep a folder with all of the documents and contracts signed. Keep a copy of every single check they write you in that file. Also, keep any correspondence you send (a copy) or receive from them in that file. You might need it one day.*

### Paying the Mortgage

Your mortgage is due every month whether the tenant-buyer pays you the rent on time or not. The tenant-buyer does have an interest in making sure that your mortgage is getting paid. If you aren't paying the mortgage it will definitely impact their ability to purchase your home down the road.

211

The mortgage is in your name, you are responsible for it getting paid, not the tenant-buyer. I definitely do not recommend allowing them to make the payment directly. If they are insistent, you can offer to send them payment verification. Be respectful of their need for verification, but also make sure you are taking the proper steps to protect yourself. I teach that it doesn't matter who is making the payment (buyer or seller) but whoever it is should give proof each month to the other one.

If you were behind on mortgage payments and had to catch them up at the time you offered your home as a rent-to-own you should probably set up an escrow payment account. The tenant-buyer pays their rent into the escrow account and the escrow pays the mortgage. If the rent isn't high enough to cover the mortgage you would also pay into the escrow to cover the difference. If there is additional money left each month it gets paid to you.

The escrow set up not only protects the tenant-buyer but it also protects you. It helps you to make sure you stay legally compliant with the option and sales contract you signed.

**Paying Utilities**

Utility accounts are connected either to a person or to the property itself. In most parts of the country they are attached to the person or can be attached to the person. This is what you want. Get them out of your name and into your tenant-buyer's name. We talked about this in Chapter 16. In the case where a utility or service is connected directly to the property (in some areas water bills), if they aren't paid you can't sell the home and the tenant-buyer can't buy the home until they are paid. Obviously, this makes it important to both of you.

If the tenant-buyer is responsible for all utility payments including ones attached to the home (which I recommend since it never seems to kill a deal and they need to get used to paying all of these bills), you would want to pay the bill yourself and then bill the tenant-buyer directly. This is the best way to guarantee for you that they are being paid.

The other option is to have them pay the bills and send you a receipt for verification. It would be pretty rare for tenant-buyers to want verification that these are paid. However, most utility bills show the previous month's balance and payment received on the current month's bill. When you submit a copy of the current month's bill to the tenant-buyer for them to pay you, they can verify that the last month was paid.

**Paying Property Taxes**

You will want to pay your own property taxes. The way to your tenant-buyer to cover this expense is not to charge them for it, but to get more per month for the rent. This is an owner type of bill and you will want to pay it on a rent-to-own, or it will look more like a seller-financed transaction. Remember the dreaded phrase, *equitable interest*? Making tenant-buyers pay the property taxes is a dead-ringer for creating *equitable interest*. Don't do it.

Again, in most cases the tenant-buyer isn't going to think to ask for verification that the taxes have been paid. But it's important that they are paid, because you can't sell the home otherwise. If the tenant-buyer does want verification, you can either send them a copy of the payment receipt or they can either use the internet or their phone to check with the local tax assessor's office.

**Paying Maintenance Fees**

Fees such as pool maintenance, lawn care, septic pumping, etc. are most likely going to be the responsibility of the tenant-buyer. You don't want to keep these in your name. However, you do want to make sure that these things are still getting done. You can hire a pool service so it is done properly, but part of their rental agreement states they pay for this bill each month or whenever it is due.

You won't be paying some of these bills directly, since the tenant-buyer holds the account. Most of them you can simply verify are being done by periodic scheduled inspection visits to the property. The ones you can't see, such as septic pumping, you may want to request a copy of the receipt. You may also want to send out an annual reminder to the tenant-buyer when the septic pumping is due. This helps make sure they remember to schedule it.

## Homeowner Association Dues (HOA)

Homeowner Association dues are typically attached to the property. If they aren't paid the HOA association can place a lien against your home to prevent you from selling it until they are paid. This is an owner type of bill, so I recommend you pay it and do not try to pass this on to the tenant-buyer.

## If You Can't Agree Try Escrow

While I said it was rare that a tenant-buyer would ask to see receipt of payment, in some cases they might want that verification. In even more rare cases, they may insist on making the payment themselves for things like your mortgage payment so they have true confirmation.

This puts you in the position of not making the payment and having to rely on the tenant-buyer. I don't recommend this, unless you agree IN WRITING that if they miss one payment or are late that all future payments go directly to you and can no longer be paid to the lender directly.

If you cannot reach an agreement with your tenant-buyer on this, you certainly don't want to let the deal fall apart. Instead I recommend setting up an escrow service. An escrow service would be a neutral third party, such as an attorney or there are escrow companies that do only this. The escrow service would then make the payment for you after they receive the funds and can then provide both you and the tenant-buyer with verification.

In the next chapter we will look at how the tenant-buyer can improve their credit so they can qualify for a mortgage and buy your home. While improving credit may not be a priority for you, it will most likely be for your tenant-buyer, and you may need to help them get it done. You don't have to pay their bills, but let's get them on the right track!

# Chapter 18

## How to Help Your Buyers

## Qualify for a Mortgage

The recent credit crunch has made qualifying for financing significantly more difficult for even those with good credit. It used to be that many rent-to-own tenant-buyers could just make on-time payments for a while and they would be able to get a mortgage.

Now this isn't enough for foreclosure-weary lenders. They want to see improved credit scores. This is why credit repair is more important than ever.

It's a good idea for you as the seller to periodically check in with your tenant-buyer to see how they are doing at improving their credit. You want to help keep them on track so that they can purchase your home down the road.

### Wendy's Wisdom

*It isn't critical for you to know everything I describe below for your tenant-buyers to qualify for a mortgage. However, it is important for them. You may even want to give them a copy of this chapter to help give them ideas about what they can do.*

### Working with a Mortgage Broker

The first important step for your tenant-buyers to take toward qualifying for a mortgage is to stay in touch with their mortgage broker. A good mortgage broker can give them an overall guideline for steps they need to take to get their credit in shape and can also help them stay on track.

215

Mortgage brokers are wired in to the changing requirements of qualifying for a mortgage and will be able to help guide your tenant-buyers through the process. Not all mortgage brokers are credit experts. Some just know how to write loans. They may be able to tell your tenant-buyers what their current credit score is and what bad marks they have.

It would be great if you know a mortgage broker or your real estate agent or tenant-buyer does, that can do both loan writing and credit repair. That gives a starting point, at least. If you want to use one of the lenders I use, you can find one on my website with the other information on rent-to-own.

## Credit Reports

It is important for a tenant-buyer to be aware of what is on their credit report and work to fix the bad marks. There are a number of factors that can cause poor credit, such as late payments, foreclosures, bankruptcy, settled debts, unpaid debts, over-extended credit and a lack of credit history.

Tenant-buyers will want to focus their efforts to maximize their credit score increase during the lease period. Let's take a look at some things they can do to improve their credit.

## Paying on Time

This is a critical step. Tenant-buyers need to make their payments on time. Not just with their monthly rent but also all of their other bills. Every bill that is a late payment is a ding against their credit score. Even with just one ding after they start renting with you, a lender may reject them. Just as late payments are damaging to credit scores, on- time payments can help boost credit scores.

## Stop Using Credit Cards

Tenant-buyers with a lot of debt or over-extended credit need to stop using their credit cards and stop accumulating other debts. If they are serious about buying a home, they need to stop accumulating other debts. They don't want to buy a new car, buy furniture on a payment plan, etc. Nothing. They need to focus on paying bills off and on time.

The more debts someone has the lower their credit score, and the lower the amount of mortgage they can qualify for – if they can qualify at all.

## Building New Credit

This applies only for tenant-buyers who don't have enough established credit accounts to qualify for a mortgage. It should NOT be used by tenant-buyers who already have established credit.

In the case of tenant-buyers who have very little credit history and need to build their credit, it can be useful to establish a couple of new credit accounts. For example, they may get a new credit card or purchase furniture with financing. I know I just said they shouldn't do that, but I'll explain.

With either type of financing they should make monthly payments to help establish a credit history. However, they should definitely PAY OFF these accounts in full at least 3 months before it comes time to apply for a mortgage. Otherwise the debts on these credit accounts may hurt their chances of getting a mortgage. A mortgage lender should help them with this, not you.

## Challenging Items on a Credit Report

Another important step toward improving credit is to challenge any items that appear on the credit report that are invalid. In cases of credit fraud or even errors, sometimes accounts appear on a credit report that don't belong to the tenant-buyer. These accounts should be challenged to get them removed.

I'll talk later about using credit repair companies that can handle this for your tenant-buyers.

## Closing Old Accounts

Tenant-buyers with long established credit histories may have numerous old accounts that are no longer used. For example, if a tenant-buyer purchased furniture with financing through a credit company, that credit company would set up an account. The account is not automatically closed when the debt is paid off. Surprisingly, it doesn't even get automatically closed if the furniture store goes out of business. However, when lenders consider how much to loan you they do take the available credit for that account into consideration-- whether you are using it or not.

It may be a good idea to close out some of these accounts, however, talk to your mortgage lender first. Sometimes closing an account can make a credit score drop. Old established accounts without any outstanding balance can help a credit score go up. Tenant-buyers will want to do this early on instead of waiting until they are close to applying for a mortgage. Strangely, if the accounts are closed too close to applying for financing, it won't help the tenant-buyers.

## Paying Off Other Debts

Many buyers are denied mortgages because they have too much other debt. Even if they can get a mortgage, the amount they can qualify for will be reduced because of the other debts.

Tenant-buyers will want to strike a balance between paying off other debts and saving for a down payment. When it comes to paying off debts, an excellent technique is to focus on the smallest debt first and then work progressively upwards.

For example, let's say a tenant-buyer has the following debts:

| Debt Type | Debt Amount | Monthly Payment |
| --- | --- | --- |
| Gas Credit Card | $325 | $24 |
| Retail/Merchant Credit Card | $615 | $40 |
| Visa | 2,200 | $70 |
| Auto | $17,500 | $395 |

We'll also say that the tenant-buyer has an extra $175 per month in income after all bills are paid, groceries bought and so forth. Some people may make the mistake of dividing that $175 between all of the debts, like an extra $15 towards the gas credit card, $20 towards the retail credit card, $30 towards the Visa and $110 towards the car payment.

In fact, this way will take forever to pay off the debts.

Others may pay the extra towards the highest interest rate debt first. This is a smart idea, but when it comes to qualifying for a mortgage there is a much better way to pay off debts. Focus on the smallest debt first and then work your way up.

In this case, the smallest debt is the gas credit card for $325. Combining the regular monthly payment of $24 with the additional $175, makes for a total payment of $199. If the tenant-buyer makes

219

the $199 payment in the first month on the gas card (and pays the minimum on all of the other balances ON-TIME) the next month's balance will be approximately $130 (because there will be some interest charged). In the second month the tenant-buyer can pay off the first debt with a payment of $130 and still have $69 left over from the $199 total.

That $69 should be applied with the $40 payment on the retail/merchant credit card for a total payment of $109 in the second month. In the third month the tenant-buyer has now paid off the gas credit card and can make a total payment of $239 towards the retail credit card, which now has a balance of $515. How did the payment go up to $239, you ask?

By paying off the smallest balance debt first, the tenant-buyer can now roll that monthly payment of $24 onto paying the next debt, so the total payment is $24 from the gas card, plus $40 from the retail credit card, plus $175 in extra funds for a total of $239.

At this rate the tenant-buyer will be able to pay off the retail credit card in just over two more months. After that, he will be able to make a total payment of $309 per month against the Visa card debt. It will take about 7 months to pay off the Visa card at that rate. In about 1 year the tenant-buyer will have paid off the gas credit card, the retail credit card and the Visa card.

## Wendy's Wisdom

*This technique is not just useful for your tenant-buyers. You can also use it yourself to pay off your own debts.*

Not only does paying off these debts help their credit but it also has two other benefits. Paying more than the minimum amount on these debts can also improve their credit score. But more importantly, the tenant-buyer has freed up $134 in monthly payments ($24 from the gas card, $40 from the retail card and $70 from the Visa card).

Eliminating those monthly payments can increase the amount of the mortgage the tenant-buyer can qualify for substantially.

For example, just eliminating the $24 payment for the gas card can increase the mortgage amount by around $4,000. Eliminate the retail credit card debt payment and the mortgage can increase by another $7,000. These amounts will depend, of course, on the interest rate of the mortgage and the monthly income of the tenant-buyer, among other things. This should give you an idea of how a small monthly payment can make a big difference on the amount financed. This is why taking on new debt is very dangerous for tenant-buyers.

**Building Up a Down Payment**

In addition to improving credit, tenant-buyers may also need to save up for a larger down payment. How much of a down payment they will need depends on the type of financing their mortgage broker can get them.

One issue to be aware of is that as the credit crunch continues, lenders may restrict financing even further. It will definitely be a benefit for tenant-buyers to have MORE of a down payment than less. However, there are still many FHA programs that might work for your tenant-buyers that have a minimal amount down.

Tenant-buyers can accumulate a down payment several ways. The option fee they paid at the beginning will be a part of their down payment. Tenant-buyers can also accumulate option credits if you allow and give them. They also have the ability to save additional money on their own as well.

This is another reason why it is good for tenant-buyers to stay in touch with their mortgage broker to know how lender's rules are changing and what they will need when it comes time to purchase your home.

In our previous example of paying off debts, we had the tenant-buyer paying off the gas credit card, the retail credit card and the Visa card. In fact, it might be better for the tenant-buyer to only pay off the gas credit card and retail credit card and continue making normal payments on the Visa card and then save the extra money for a down payment.

On an 18-month rent-to-own option, it took the first 5 months to pay off the two smaller accounts. After that the tenant-buyer would be able to save $239 per month for 13 months, or a total of another $3,100. This might be more beneficial than paying off the Visa card.

All of this will be a plan they should develop with their mortgage lender. As I already said however, many lenders do not understand and know how to work with a rent-to-own buyer. To find a good lender to recommend to your tenant-buyer, go to www.WendyPatton.com and go to the Rent-to-Own site for information on a mortgage lender in your area.

## Wendy's Wisdom

*Require your tenant-buyer to get into credit repair, if they have credit issues, as part of the Option Agreement. You might need to collect an extra $100 per month to cover the expense or reduce their option fee by the amount needed for credit repair, and get them signed up. It will pay off for you and your tenant-buyer later.*

**Credit Repair**

There are also credit repair companies that will help the tenant-buyer with credit repair. They specialize in repair and some will guarantee results. Most of the time credit repair companies are necessary to help your tenant-buyer. They know the laws and loopholes that will get some, if not all derogatory information off of someone's credit. I have seen them get bankruptcies, foreclosures, collection accounts, etc. off a person's credit report. You can check out: www.RenttoOwnCreditRepair.com to get more information.

If your tenant-buyers take the necessary steps they should be able to qualify for a mortgage and purchase your home. Sometimes things don't always work out as planned and the tenant-buyer needs more time, or some other problem crops up. In the next chapter we look at how to handle problems that might occur when selling your home on a rent-to-own.

# Chapter 19

# Oops, Not Everything Went to Plan

Even the best laid plans and the best intentions sometimes go awry. Circumstances outside the control of you or the tenant-buyer can change. Sometimes the intentions aren't the best and you may need to take action.

This chapter isn't intended to scare you, it's meant to help you be ready in case something doesn't go as planned. Hopefully, you won't need anything in this chapter. However, in some cases you might and that is when you can use the following information to help guide you.

## Extensions

In some cases the tenant-buyer wants to buy your home, but their credit score hasn't improved enough to qualify for a mortgage. They need to extend the lease period. It is up to you whether or not to grant the extension. In most cases you would want to.

However, in granting an extension, you are also able to modify terms or ask for additional money. After all, you are giving up a large concession by giving them more time. It's only reasonable to ask for something in return, but you need to make sure that these things make sense at the time. For instance, if the value hasn't gone up on the house, then raising the price would not be wise or fair.

Several options are:

1. *Increasing the sale price* – if the housing market has appreciated in your area, you may want to increase the sales price of your home. If your market has depreciated, this probably won't work. You might actually need to decrease it a little to still get your home sold, but you can always decrease it later. No need to do so at the time you extend the contract with your tenant-buyer. You can always reduce your price when they are ready to close on your home.

2. *Increasing the option fee* – you can also ask for additional option fee money. This would apply against the purchase price when they buy, but helps give you additional security by making sure they have more invested, and will be less likely to walk away. This is non-refundable, so why not get more if they have it. Sometimes they do, but many times they don't have more money to put down.

3. *Increasing the rent* – if rental rates in your area have gone up (or even if they haven't) you may be able to increase the rent. Modest rental increases are typically only considered nuisance increases and are not enough to prompt the renter to move. But even a $20 per month rent increase is an extra $240 per year for you.

4. *Decreasing option credits* – if you had granted option credits during the initial lease period, you can have them gradually

go away during the extension. This effectively amounts to a price increase for you, but it also helps motivate the tenant-buyer to get a mortgage as quickly as possible, because they are losing money every month. However, if your tenant-buyer needs a certain amount for a down payment, reducing option credits may drop them below that amount and prevent them from obtaining a mortgage.

What you must also consider is if you have time available before you must close on your home due to capital gains issues. Check what the rules are when you sell your home, but at the time of the writing of this book, you had to live in your home for 2 out of 5 years to get the tax free exclusion on gains of $250,000 for a single person and $500,000 for a married couple. If this will affect you, then you need to make sure you will not have to pay on those gains, but if it doesn't affect you, or affect you much, no worry.

The extension details should be put into writing and signed by both you and the tenant-buyer. This prevents misunderstandings and gives you legal protection. Make sure you itemize all changes, including how long the extension is valid. Additionally, if the extension paperwork is more than one page, the tenant-buyer should initial every page. Usually it will be just a few sentences to explain what changed or what you are agreeing to, but make sure it is in writing for all parties to be protected.

**Buying with Changes**

In some cases the tenant-buyer is able to buy at the end of the initial option period but either needs or wants to renegotiate certain points of the sale.

For example, if the appraisal from the lender comes in too low for the home, the tenant-buyer may request that the purchase price be reduced. This might happen in cases where a housing market has continued to depreciate during the lease period. Unfortunately, the market is what it is and you will have to make a decision if you want to sell or not. You entered into the deal because you wanted to sell your home. Now you have to decide if you want to sell it for less. The choice is yours. Just keep in mind that the price will be the same if you try to sell it to someone else.

The closing costs from the lender may be higher than the tenant-buyer originally anticipated. They may request a seller concession to help cover those closing costs.

There may also be condition issues with your home that the tenant-buyer was not aware of initially, but learned about while living there during the lease period and they may request a reduced price to help cover them. In other cases, they may try to renegotiate the price simply because they want to try to pay less.

In ALL of these cases you are NOT obligated to give any concessions at all. The original agreement has all of the terms set forth. HOWEVER, it may be necessary to make concessions depending on what has happened with your real estate market and how badly you need or want to sell your home.

If your real estate market has declined and the tenant-buyer is asking for a price reduction, you need to face the fact that you will have to sell your home for less no matter who you sell it to. When you factor in the amount of time it may take to find a new buyer, it could end up costing you more while you make payments on your empty home.

In any situation where the tenant-buyer is simply trying to negotiate a better deal for themselves, you need to factor in your situation. Has your market appreciated or declined? How long would it take you to find a new buyer? How badly do you need to get your home sold now?

If your market has appreciated, you can tell the tenant-buyer that the original agreement stands or they can move out and forfeit their option fee. If the market hasn't been so good, you may be better off negotiating with them, giving away some small concessions to still get your home sold.

The great news in all of this: you are in control to decide what to do at this point.

The only time you don't have control is when they decide to exercise the option at the original terms and buy your home, then you must sell it to them.

**Choosing Not to Exercise the Option**

Sometimes the tenant-buyer simply decides they don't want to buy your home. Either they decided your home wasn't right for them or becoming homeowners wasn't right for them. Whatever the circumstances, they have decided to move on.

If this is the case and you have used my contracts, they are supposed to notify you in writing before the option period expires. Once you receive this notification, you can start making plans for getting your home back on the market and moving forward again.

There are some things you'll need to keep in mind:

- *Option Fee* – The option fee is non-refundable. As long as you lived up to your obligations in the contracts, it belongs to you. In rare circumstances a tenant-buyer may try to recover the option fee through a legal avenue. My contracts have held up in court and been very successful on the rare occasion they were tested. This is why good contracts are so important. You don't want the ones from the local office supply store for when so much is at stake.

- *Condition of the home* – Your home is supposed to be returned to you in the condition it was in when the tenant-buyer moved in, less normal wear and tear. If there are damages to your home, it is the tenant-buyer's obligation to fix them or be financially responsible for them. Any security deposit you collected would apply against damages or unpaid rent. Any deductions you take against the security

229

deposit need to be itemized to the tenant in writing. If there is a security deposit balance left it needs to be returned to the tenant-buyer.

If the damages exceed the security deposit you can sue the tenant-buyer for the balance. These types of lawsuits have varying success. Sometimes they work and you get your money, but sometimes you win the suit and are unable to collect the money. You will need to decide if the amount of damage is worth pursuing in court. Usually Small Claims Court is what you need and you don't need an attorney – it's usually easy to file.

- *When to put your home back on the market* – According to my contracts, you are entitled to put your home back on the market 30 days before the tenant-buyer moves out. Any showings of the home to future tenant-buyers must be scheduled in advance and sufficient notice - usually 24 hours - provided to the existing tenant.

Depending on the condition of your home you will need to decide if you want to put it on the market before the current tenant moves out. If your home is in good shape and kept clean, you'll want to get it on the market right away. If the tenant isn't taking very good care of it and it doesn't show well you may want to wait until after they have moved out.

Typically it is better to show a home with furnishings in it than to show an empty home, provided it shows well.

## Evictions

Sometimes if a tenant-buyer stops paying the rent or breaks another rule it becomes necessary to evict them. The main reason you will end up evicting someone is if they didn't pay their rent.

Before I go into details on evictions, this is a good point to remind you that if you use a property manager to manage your home, you won't have to deal with this. If a tenant is late with their rent the property manager takes the appropriate steps. If it becomes necessary to evict, either the property manager can handle the eviction or can recommend an eviction attorney. This maintains a degree of separation between you and the tenants, which greatly reduces headaches for you if things go wrong.

Here's the thing, tenants that stop paying rent or break other rules will lie to you. They will make up story after story if you let them. Once a tenant has stopped paying rent they will often milk as much "free" living time out of you as they can. The thing is, it's not free. It's coming out of your pocket every month.

## Wendy's Wisdom

*There is only one of two people paying your payment - you or your tenant-buyer. You decide which one you want to pay it.*

I'm going to give you an extreme example of how bad a tenant lie can be. It's December 3rd and you haven't received the rent check yet. You try calling the tenant a few times but don't hear back from them, so you go to the house on December the 10th. The tenant is there and tells you how embarrassed they are that they can't pay. Her husband just lost his job. If you can please just be a little patient with them, she's trying to get the money from her family so they can stay while her husband looks for a job.

She promises to call you in a couple of days when she knows more. Three days later you don't hear back. You call and she tells you it looks like her parents will be sending her a check so she can cover the rent, and she asks you to wait until the check arrives so she can pay you. A week goes by and it's now December 20th and you haven't heard back from the tenants yet. So you call again. This time the husband answers. He says he is terribly sorry, but it doesn't look like her parents will be sending money until after Christmas. "But," he says, "I've got a couple of good leads on jobs." When you tell him that if you don't have the money right away, you'll have to start the eviction, he pleads with you not to put his family out right before Christmas. "Plus, we just found out that my wife is pregnant with another baby." Sucker that you are, you agree to let them stay.

The beginning of January rolls around, and the tenant is now two payments behind. You again ask for the rent and they give you a check. The husband says he'll be working again soon.

Seven days later the check bounces. Irate, you call up the tenants and the wife is almost sobbing saying how sorry she is. But she says her husband has started working again, so he'll get his first check in three weeks, and then they can start paying you again. Three and a half weeks later you still don't have any money. You call the tenant once again. The tenants say they were just going to call you, and they have some money, but not too much since the first paycheck was for only one week. They want to know if you would be willing to accept $200 in cash as a first payment so they can start getting caught up again. You collect the cash and they tell you that in another two weeks he'll have another check, and they can give you another payment.

Two and a half weeks later and you're now into February and they are three payments behind. The two hundred you received from them doesn't cover the bounced check fee and all of the late fees. You call the tenants again and no answer. You call a couple of more times and still nothing. So you go to the home and the wife starts to cry, her husband's new job didn't work out. They let him go. She's crying, saying that it's the middle of February, her husband hasn't found a job and she is five months pregnant and they have nowhere to go.

Need I go on?

Start the eviction as soon as they don't pay. Tell them in the beginning this is your process and not to take it personally even if you agree to let them pay later. It protects you in case they don't pay. If you want to find a reasonable attorney to evict someone, go to your local real estate investor group or call them to see if they have someone they can recommend that is good and reasonable.

## Wendy's Wisdom

*Don't let this story scare you. Remember two things:*
*1. Evictions are rare.*
*2. If you do evict, it doesn't have to be anywhere near this bad.*
*If you read on you'll see another way the story can play out simply by you taking appropriate action that works out MUCH better for the landlord.*

If you were the landlord in this situation you would never really know how much of what they are telling you is the truth. It could be all true, or absolutely none of it could be true. What happens if the landlord (you) starts the eviction proceedings at this point in the story, even in the quickest states for evictions, the tenants won't be out until March and they'll owe you four months of past due rent. In other states it can take even longer. They could be in the house for a couple of more months before you can finally evict them.

The end result is that you will be paying for them to live for free in your home with all of the money coming out of your pocket. Not to mention all of the headaches and stress on your end of trying to get a hold of the tenant and trying to get the rent from them.

Here is another way the story can play out. Roll back the clock and it's the 3rd of December and the rent hasn't arrived. In Michigan you would send the "7 Day Notice to Quit" to the tenant by mail on the 4th. In many states it is a 3 day notice; some a 4 day notice, etc. This is free to send, and you can get them free, or close to free, at your courthouse or a property management office. This is the first step to eviction. You don't have to follow all the way through with the eviction if the tenant pays, but this allows you to start on it right away. You also call the tenant-buyer to find out why the rent is late, but don't hear back from them.

When the "7 Day Notice to Quit" arrives in the tenant-buyer's mail THEY call YOU (nice change from you having to constantly call, huh?). They relay the same sob story as above and you tell them that you are very sorry to hear about the troubles they are having, and hope they'll be able to come up with the rent money. You tell them that they have until the 12th (7 days, after the "7 Day Notice to Quit" was mailed).

If you don't have the rent in hand by the 12th (or the day it is due in your state), your eviction attorney files the eviction notice at the court. At that time you can send a notice, in writing, to the tenant-buyer that their option has been revoked, if you choose, due to the rent being more than 10 days late. The tenant-buyer usually has all the way up until the eviction hearing (plus what a judge grants them) to pay you the rent plus late charges. If they are unable to pay in full, they can be evicted.

## Warning

*Don't send them a notice that you will revoke their option, unless you really want them out. I usually work with people until I know they can't or won't pay. You can always send that notice later, if you choose.*

**Your Goal** →

**Remember your Goal:
Get your home SOLD!**

See how much quicker that is? Not listening to the stories saves you about three months worth of missing rent payments. You can listen, you just need to proceed down the path of eviction until the payment is in hand. I know it sounds a little heartless, but the reality is that you have no idea how much of their story is true. It really doesn't matter how much is true. The contract between you and the tenant-buyer is that you provide them with a place to live if they pay the rent. If they don't live up to their end of the bargain you MUST evict them. You'll end up doing it sooner or later, but if you end up doing it later it's going to cost you a whole lot more money.

Do the math: 3 months @ $1,000 per month = $3,000. Does $3,000 out of your pocket justify starting the eviction process?

When it comes to evictions, the only way to do it is quickly and legally. Eviction laws vary state-to-state and sometimes even city-to-city, so it isn't possible for me to outline all of the steps specific for you.

I do recommend that you hire an eviction attorney. They don't usually cost too much and it takes a LOT of headache and stress out of the process for you. Not only that, but it makes sure that you do everything legally. With your Pre-Paid Legal membership you can also ask for an attorney's advice (no charge) or an attorney to do the eviction for you at a discount.

## Wendy's Wisdom

*Hire an eviction attorney! Don't do this yourself. Trust me on this one.*

If you have to evict a tenant-buyer, it is best not to put your home back on the market until AFTER the tenant-buyer is out of the home. If you try to do showings while the tenant-buyer still occupies the home, you'll have nothing but problems.

A final note on evictions – the option fee does NOT count towards rent. What I mean is if a tenant is late with the rent and they say to take if off the option fee - it doesn't work that way. The option fee money is yours, it's non-refundable. The only way the tenant-buyer can get it back is by buying the house and having it credited towards the purchase price. Also, do not agree to add the late rent to the purchase price so they don't have to pay. If they don't pay the rent, they won't be able to get a mortgage and they'll never be able to buy your home. So agreeing to add the rent to the purchase price means you just agreed to let them live in your home for free.

**Putting Your Home Back on the Market**

In any situation where the tenant-buyer is not purchasing your home, you will need to put it back on the market. In some cases you can put it back on the market before the tenant-buyer moves out; in other cases you will need to wait until after they have moved out. No matter what the case is, you will want to take some steps to make sure you are putting it back on the market correctly.

You should make sure the home is properly cleaned. The carpets should be cleaned. Any holes or dings in the walls should be repaired and the paint should look fresh. The kitchens and baths should be scrubbed spotless and so on. It's the same as preparing the home the first time around. You want it to look just as good. If there were any damages to your home by the previous tenants you will need to repair those as well. Do some staging of the home like the first time.

You also want to change the locks. This is a must for security and legal protection. You should do this any time there is a change in who lives in the home – even when you move out. This way there is no question later if someone got in and it was your old locks. Who did you give the key to before? Why didn't you take precautions? You get the idea.

You will want to get an accurate price for your home in the current market. Given the amount of time your previous tenant was living there, your home may have gone up or down in value.

Get your marketing back up and running and decide whether to list your home with a real estate agent. Refer back to Chapter 7 for the different marketing techniques.

Not having a tenant-buyer exercise their option and purchase your home can be both disappointing and frustrating. However, it does happen sometimes. When you are putting your home back on the market you need to get a fresh start. If you don't take all of the steps that you took the first time around, you'll be selling yourself short and making it much more difficult to find the next tenant-buyer.

If it doesn't work out with the first one, find another so you can get your home sold. In the next chapter we'll talk about the closing, when your home is finally getting sold.

# Chapter 20

## Completing the Transaction and Selling Your Home

You made it! It's time to sell your home to your tenant-buyer. Congratulations!

When it comes time to close, there are some things that are helpful to know, particularly with the HUD-1 settlement statement and some tax implications. The HUD-1 statement contains all of the numbers for your closing and will show how much money you will be receiving or giving at the closing (well, hopefully receiving). Fortunately this isn't too complicated, because you can always ask questions and ask for help from your closing agent, real estate agent or attorney.

Below is a blank copy of the HUD-1 settlement statement for you to reference as I will talk about some sections on the HUD-1 in this chapter that are important for you.

The HUD-1 settlement statement details where all of the money is going. The HUD-1 (or HUD as it is commonly called) is mandatory everywhere in the country as required in Section 4 of RESPA (Real Estate Settlement and Procedures Act).

According to RESPA you are supposed to be given a copy of the HUD-1 at least one day prior to closing. Unfortunately this doesn't always happen if the title company or attorney gets stuck waiting for paperwork from other sources.

The HUD-1 is very important to you. It covers all of the financial details of the sale of your home, including how much money you will get or have to pay (if you owe more than you are selling for) at closing.

Here is the thing about the HUD-1: mistakes can happen. It's very important for you to review the HUD-1 (preferably with your real estate agent or attorney) to make sure it's accurate. Rent-to-own home sales are a bit more complex and unusual compared to the average real estate transaction, so the closing agent that prepares the HUD-1 may miss something. Check everything that you can. Confirm how much your buyer paid, how much credit you gave them, and any other provisions in your agreement. Make sure they are all reflected accurately.

**A. Settlement Statement**

**U.S. Department of Housing and Urban Development**

OMB Approval No. 2502-0265
(expires 11/30/2009)

---

**B. Type of Loan**

| | | | |
|---|---|---|---|
| 1. ☐ FHA | 2. ☐ FmHA | 3. ☐ Conv. Unins. | 6. File Number: |
| 4. ☐ VA | 5. ☐ Conv. Ins. | | 7. Loan Number: |

8. Mortgage Insurance Case Number:

**C. Note:** This form is furnished to give you a statement of actual settlement costs. Amounts paid to and by the settlement agent are shown. Items marked "(p.o.c.)" were paid outside the closing; they are shown here for informational purposes and are not included in the totals.

| D. Name & Address of Borrower: | E. Name & Address of Seller: | F. Name & Address of Lender: |
|---|---|---|
| | | d |

| G. Property Location: | H. Settlement Agent: | |
|---|---|---|
| | Place of Settlement: | I. Settlement Date: |

---

| **J. Summary of Borrower's Transaction** | | **K. Summary of Seller's Transaction** | |
|---|---|---|---|
| **100. Gross Amount Due From Borrower** | | **400. Gross Amount Due To Seller** | |
| 101. Contract sales price | | 401. Contract sales price | |
| 102. Personal property | | 402. Personal property | |
| 103. Settlement charges to borrower (line 1400) | | 403. | |
| 104. | | 404. | |
| 105. | | 405. | |
| **Adjustments for items paid by seller in advance** | | **Adjustments for items paid by seller in advance** | |
| 106. City/town taxes to | | 406. City/town taxes to | |
| 107. County taxes to | | 407. County taxes to | |
| 108. Assessments to | | 408. Assessments to | |
| 109. | | 409. | |
| 110. | | 410. | |
| 111. | | 411. | |
| 112. | | 412. | |
| **120. Gross Amount Due From Borrower** | | **420. Gross Amount Due To Seller** | |
| **200. Amounts Paid By Or In Behalf Of Borrower** | | **500. Reductions In Amount Due To Seller** | |
| 201. Deposit or earnest money | | 501. Excess deposit (see instructions) | |
| 202. Principal amount of new loan(s) | | 502. Settlement charges to seller (line 1400) | |
| 203. Existing loan(s) taken subject to | | 503. Existing loan(s) taken subject to | |
| 204. | | 504. Payoff of first mortgage loan | |
| 205. | | 505. Payoff of second mortgage loan | |
| 206. | | 506. | |
| 207. | | 507. | |
| 208. | | 508. | |
| 209. | | 509. | |
| **Adjustments for items unpaid by seller** | | **Adjustments for items unpaid by seller** | |
| 210. City/town taxes to | | 510. City/town taxes to | |
| 211. County taxes to | | 511. County taxes to | |
| 212. Assessments to | | 512. Assessments to | |
| 213. | | 513. | |
| 214. | | 514. | |
| 215. | | 515. | |
| 216. | | 516. | |
| 217. | | 517. | |
| 218. | | 518. | |
| 219. | | 519. | |
| **220. Total Paid By/For Borrower** | | **520. Total Reduction Amount Due Seller** | |
| **300. Cash At Settlement From/To Borrower** | | **600. Cash At Settlement To/From Seller** | |
| 301. Gross Amount due from borrower (line 120) | | 601. Gross amount due to seller (line 420) | |
| 302. Less amounts paid by/for borrower (line 220) | ( ) | 602. Less reductions in amt. due seller (line 520) | ( ) |
| **303. Cash** ☐ From ☐ To Borrower | | **603. Cash** ☐ To ☐ From Seller | 0.00 |

---

Section 5 of the Real Estate Settlement Procedures Act (RESPA) requires the following: • HUD must develop a Special Information Booklet to help persons borrowing money to finance the purchase of residential real estate to better understand the nature and costs of real estate settlement services; • Each lender must provide the booklet to all applicants from whom it receives or for whom it prepares a written application to borrow money to finance the purchase of residential real estate; • Lenders must prepare and distribute with the Booklet a Good Faith Estimate of the settlement costs that the borrower is likely to incur in connection with the settlement. These disclosures are mandatory.

Section 4(a) of RESPA mandates that HUD develop and prescribe this standard form to be used at the time of loan settlement to provide full disclosure of all charges imposed upon the borrower and seller. These are third party disclosures that are designed to provide the borrower with pertinent information during the settlement process in order to be a better shopper.

The Public Reporting Burden for this collection of information is estimated to average one hour per response, including the time for reviewing instructions, searching existing data sources, gathering and maintaining the data needed, and completing and reviewing the collection of information.

This agency may not collect this information, and you are not required to complete this form, unless it displays a currently valid OMB control number.

The information requested does not lend itself to confidentiality.

*Wendy Patton*

**L. Settlement Charges**

| | | | Paid From Borrowers Funds at Settlement | Paid From Seller's Funds at Settlement |
|---|---|---|---|---|
| **700. Total Sales/Broker's Commission based on price $** @ % = | | | | |
| Division of Commission (line 700) as follows: | | | | |
| 701. $ to | | | | |
| 702. $ to | | | | |
| 703. Commission paid at Settlement | | | | |
| 704. | | | | |
| **800. Items Payable In Connection With Loan** | | | | |
| 801. Loan Origination Fee % | | | | |
| 802. Loan Discount % | | | | |
| 803. Appraisal Fee to | | | | |
| 804. Credit Report to | | | | |
| 805. Lender's Inspection Fee | | | | |
| 806. Mortgage Insurance Application Fee to | | | | |
| 807. Assumption Fee | | | | |
| 808. | | | | |
| 809. | | | | |
| 810. | | | | |
| 811. | | | | |
| **900. Items Required By Lender To Be Paid In Advance** | | | | |
| 901. Interest from to @$ /day | | | | |
| 902. Mortgage Insurance Premium for months to | | | | |
| 903. Hazard Insurance Premium for years to | | | | |
| 904. years to | | | | |
| 905. | | | | |
| **1000. Reserves Deposited With Lender** | | | | |
| 1001. Hazard insurance months@$ per month | | | | |
| 1002. Mortgage insurance months@$ per month | | | | |
| 1003. City property taxes months@$ per month | | | | |
| 1004. County property taxes months@$ per month | | | | |
| 1005. Annual assessments months@$ per month | | | | |
| 1006. months@$ per month | | | | |
| 1007. months@$ per month | | | | |
| 1008. months@$ per month | | | | |
| **1100. Title Charges** | | | | |
| 1101. Settlement or closing fee to | | | | |
| 1102. Abstract or title search to | | | | |
| 1103. Title examination to | | | | |
| 1104. Title insurance binder to | | | | |
| 1105. Document preparation to | | | | |
| 1106. Notary fees to | | | | |
| 1107. Attorney's fees to | | | | |
| (includes above items numbers: ) | | | | |
| 1108. Title insurance to | | | | |
| (includes above items numbers: ) | | | | |
| 1109. Lender's coverage $ | | | | |
| 1110. Owner's coverage $ | | | | |
| 1111. | | | | |
| 1112. | | | | |
| 1113. | | | | |
| **1200. Government Recording and Transfer Charges** | | | | |
| 1201. Recording fees: Deed $ ; Mortgage $ ; Releases $ | | | | |
| 1202. City/county tax/stamps: Deed $ ; Mortgage $ | | | | |
| 1203. State tax/stamps: Deed $ ; Mortgage $ | | | | |
| 1204. | | | | |
| 1205. | | | | |
| **1300. Additional Settlement Charges** | | | | |
| 1301. Survey to | | | | |
| 1302. Pest inspection to | | | | |
| 1303. | | | | |
| 1304. | | | | |
| 1305. | | | | |
| **1400. Total Settlement Charges (enter on lines 103, Section J and 502, Section K)** | | | | |

242

## Wendy's Wisdom

*Don't let the HUD-1 intimidate you.*
*Ask for help from your real estate agent or attorney.*

**The Closing**

This is where your home is officially sold. Your tenant-buyer has a mortgage and the deed/title of the home is transferred to them.

Closings can be confusing for the average buyer or seller because they are asked to sign a lot of paperwork, but don't always understand what they are signing. You can always ask questions about anything you don't understand. Prior to the closing, if you haven't signed up for Pre-Paid Legal, you will want to do so now. Your Pre-Paid Legal attorney can review all of your closing documents with you. There is usually no charge for this service.

You can sign up at www.prepaidlegal.com/hub/wendypatton.

When you go to the closing there is a mountain of paperwork. Fortunately for you, most of it is for the buyer. You probably remember that mountain of paperwork from when you purchased your home. There will be some key documents that you'll sign, namely the title/deed and the HUD-1 settlement statement.

## Warranty Deed

The *Warranty Deed* is the piece of paper that officially transfers ownership from you to the tenant-buyer. Once this document is signed and you have received your check for closing, you have officially sold your home.

## Wendy's Wisdom

*Check the HUD-1 for mistakes. Make sure the numbers match what you think they are supposed to be. If they don't, make sure you ask why not.*

You don't have to be an expert to catch mistakes. Here are some key areas to look for in the HUD-1 (these numbers correspond to the section numbers that appear on the HUD-1):

- *101 & 401 – Contract Sales Price.* These should match each other and should be the amount shown on your sales contract with the tenant-buyer.

- *106, 107 & 406, 407 – Property Taxes on the City and County level.* Taxes are prorated based on what you agree with the tenant-buyer in the purchase agreement. Title offices are accustomed to standard purchase agreements. If you negotiate something different, it may be overlooked. In most states, property taxes are paid in arrears, and therefore you would need to pay the taxes through the date of closing. Meaning, the taxes would be pro-rated until that date for your portion and the tenant-buyer's portion. In most of Michigan taxes are paid in advance, therefore you would be credited the pro-rated taxes back, based on the HUD.

- *603 – Cash Due to/from Seller.* This is how much you will receive (or have to pay if you owe more than you are selling

244

for) at the closing. This is the final payment to you for your home. All the numbers on the HUD roll down to this number on the front page of the HUD, but it can include numbers from the second page, as well. The HUD is a two page document.

- *701/702 – Real Estate Commissions*. If you paid any commission in advance to your real estate agent make sure they are deducted from this amount.

**A Note About POC**

You may see several areas marked with the letters POC, this means Paid Outside of Closing. You want to make sure you see the option fee and any additional option credits indicated on the HUD-1. If you paid any real estate commissions in advance they should appear as your credit on the HUD-1.

**Title Insurance**

When you sell your home, you purchase title insurance. Title insurance is an insurance policy that protects the title/deed of your home. The title insurance is both necessary and a protection for you. Should there arise any problems with the title, this insurance policy is your protection. For instance: two years later your old mortgage still shows up as a lien on the tenant-buyers title (now they are the owners). The title insurance company will remove that for you. You don't have to worry about it.

Title insurance usually includes some exclusions or things that are not covered under the policy. Schedule A of the policy includes standard exclusions and Schedule B includes non-standard exclusions.

The non-standard, Schedule B exclusions will be specific to your home. You will want to review these more carefully.

You can, and should, request a copy of the title commitment prior to closing. If you have any questions don't hesitate to ask your closing agent. The title commitment is used before closing, so that anything that needs to be removed or cleaned up before the closing can be, in order to issue the final title policy for your buyer.

Depending on when you bought your home, you may have received a title insurance policy as the buyer. These insurance policies usually have value. Depending on how old the insurance policy is, you may be eligible for a credit against the cost for the new title insurance policy you are purchasing for your buyer. Make sure you show your closing agent a copy of your old title insurance policy BEFORE the closing so that they can issue you an appropriate credit. In most cases you will need to provide it when you hire a title company or an attorney to do the closing. So, go dig that old policy up in your closing documents. It could be worth hundreds of dollars for you.

## Wendy's Wisdom

*Your existing title insurance policy has value. You can receive a credit of hundreds of dollars or more for your old policy.*
*Dig it up and show it to the closing agent before the closing.*

Each state differs as to who does the title insurance policy and who executes the closing. Some states are "attorney closing" states and others are "title company" states. In either case, the title insurance is reviewed and signed off by an attorney. You will most likely have an inkling of this from when you bought your home, and you might have already bought your new home and have been through the closing process several times.

### Tax Implications

If you sell your home and make a profit, you may be subject to capital gains tax. Uncle Sam always wants his cut, but fortunately there are some ways to reduce or eliminate the tax on this income.

### *Capital Gains Exclusion*

The Capital Gains Exclusion was passed in 1997. It allows for a single person to be tax exempt on $250,000 in profit from the sale of their primary residence and a married couple to be exempt on $500,000.

The profit is not just how much you receive at closing. Profit is the NET GAIN to you after you deduct your original purchase price plus the cost of any improvements you made from the end sales price. For example, if you originally bought your home for $150,000 and spent another $35,000 remodeling the kitchen and putting on a new roof, you would have a cost on the home of $185,000. If you sold it for $250,000 your net gain would be $65,000 – TAX FREE.

The Capital Gains Exclusion is great, but there are two rules to qualify:

- First, you must live in the home for 2 years out of the last 5 years. This means you could not have rented it or have moved out for 1 day more than 3 years. This is something to consider before you do your option agreement with your tenant-buyer. You don't want to give them too much time to buy your home. If you have a large gain on your home, and you lose your right to use the capital gains exclusion, you may have to pay some taxes to Uncle Sam.

- Second, you must own the home for a minimum of 2 years. This may sound a little confusing when I already said you must live in the home for at least 2 of 5 years. The capital gains exclusion can actually be used every 2 years if you were to buy and sell your primary residence every 2 years. So, you technically only need to own and live in the home for a minimum of 2 years. But, since you are selling on a rent-to-own basis you need more time than that, since you will have a tenant-buyer living in the home for a while before it's actually sold.

This is where the 5 years comes in. The 5 year part is actually the window of opportunity. Let me give you an example to clarify. If you bought your home on July 1st of 2006 and lived in it for 2 years until June 30th of 2008, whereupon a tenant-buyer moved in, you would have lived in the home and owned the home for 2 years; thereby qualifying for the capital gains exclusion. HOWEVER, you must sell the home within a total of 5 years from the start of your 2 years of living in the home. In other words, you have 3 years LEFT to complete the sale of your home, so it must be sold by June 30th of 2011 (that's 5 years from when you first started living there).

Fortunately there is some flexibility in how these rules work. An important one for us rent-to-own home sellers is that you DON'T have to live in the home at the time when it's sold. As long as you lived in it for at least 2 of the last 5 years you qualify. Talk to your tax preparer or a tax attorney (maybe one with Pre-Paid Legal) to get the latest information on capital gains and what applies to your primary residence.

## IMPORTANT NOTE

*With the passage of certain recent housing laws, there may be changes to the capital gains exclusion rule, unless Congress makes additional changes. Before you make any tax decisions regarding the sale of your home, check with your tax advisor for the most current information.*

## Other Tax Considerations

### *Rental Income*

If the rental income you receive from the tenant-buyer exceeds the amount of your monthly costs on the property (mortgage payments, taxes, insurance, etc.) you may have to pay income taxes on the additional income.

However, during the time your property is a rental you can also depreciate the property on your federal taxes to help offset this income. The standard depreciation rule is 27.5 years, meaning that you can depreciate the total value of a rental property (excluding the land) over a period of 27.5 years. If your home is worth $150,000 (after deducting the land, which isn't depreciable), you would be able to take a depreciation deduction of approximately, $5,450 per year that you are renting your home. You can deduct this amount against rental income that you receive, but you can only take as much of the depreciation deduction as you need. For example, if you are renting your home for $1,250 per month, but your mortgage payment, taxes, and insurance are $1,150 per month, that gives you $100 per month in positive cash flow, or $1,200 per year. This means you would take only $1,200 out of the available $5,450 depreciation deduction and you would pay no taxes on the rental income.

Note, however, that if you do take the depreciation deduction during the rental period you WILL NOT be able to claim the depreciated amount as part of your capital gains exclusion. You will want to talk with your tax advisor BEFORE you take the rental depreciation deduction to determine the best strategy for you with regards to depreciation and the capital gains exclusion.

## Wendy's Wisdom

*Taxes are complicated. Adding a rental property into the mix makes it more complicated. Get help from a tax professional to determine your personal best strategy.*

### *Option Fees*

If you collect option fees from a tenant-buyer that chooses not to exercise the option (in other words, they don't buy your home) those option fees are subject to income tax. The option fee you received would need to be declared as ordinary income in the year the option expires (although you may be able to deduct any costs such as real estate commissions or advertising fees). Again, check with your tax advisor.

That's it! With your rent-to-own home now sold, you can move on with your life, hopefully pocket some extra money by getting a better purchase price for your home by selling it on a rent-to-own.

In the next chapter I will go over some odds and ends you'll want to make sure you get right during the rent-to-own process that will help you maintain your sanity.

# Chapter 21

## Important Components to Get Right So You Can Maintain Your Sanity

This chapter is full of practical advice to make your rent-to-own experience easier and better for you. It comes largely from mistakes that I and my fellow colleagues have made. Following this advice won't guarantee you a problem free rent-to-own experience, but it will definitely help manage a lot of the factors that can lead to problems.

**Don't Compromise Your Qualification List**

When it comes time to place a tenant-buyer, we sometimes feel pressured to get someone in as quickly as possible. This usually happens because the mortgage payment for your home has become a financial burden.

Even if that is the case, you still need to make sure that when you screen your tenant-buyer they meet the criteria on your qualifications list. Failing to do so can cause you problems for two reasons:

1. It could be a violation of Fair Housing Law

2. You could end up placing a bad tenant and have to evict them later. Don't go by gut feel. Approve a person because they meet your qualifications.

*Story from Wendy: I was only 21 or 22 at the time I had my first two rental homes. I was a single woman and showed my properties alone. One day I was showing one of my homes and up drove two big guys with long hair on Harleys. I was alone in the home and was a bit nervous, to say the least, but showed the guys around the home. They really wanted the home and filled out an application.*

*I don't remember the details, but I remember they were very polite and professional when I met them. They also met my qualifications and I approved them. They turned out to be the best paying, cleanest tenants a landlord could hope for. They were total gems, and I wish all of my tenants and tenant-buyers were like them. I was naïve at that age and didn't know much, but I am glad I didn't judge them based on how they first appeared. I later found out that Harley riders, on average, have a pretty decent income. I guess they would have to considering how much those bikes cost.*

*Here's another example from when I was just getting started: I had this very nice young couple, with a nice car and clean cut children drive up to see one of my rental homes. I was immediately excited by the "look of them." They ended up wanting the home and I approved them. They turned out to be the biggest pain in my behind. They didn't pay right, they always complained about everything in the home, and it turned out I had to later evict them for not paying their rent.*

*When they left the home it was a pigsty. I will admit to you, I didn't have any other applicants so I didn't do such a thorough job screening them. I screwed up.*

I share these stories with you because it would have been better if I was blind and deaf when approving some of my past tenants. It is all about setting standards and qualifications – so stick to them!

## Screen Your Prospective Tenant-Buyers

Not screening your tenant-buyers usually happens like failing to stick with your tenant-qualifications list - when you feel the pressure of your mortgage payment beating down on you. Going with your gut so you can get someone in quick to start covering your mortgage payment is a recipe for disaster.

Sometimes prospective tenant-buyers have very believable stories why they need to move in quickly. Here is another example. I had one tenant-buyer who had been living with her mom and told me she had to be out this weekend (it was a Friday already). She had cash and was ready to move in. Stupidly, I let her move in. That first month's cash was the only full month rent I ever saw from her. For the next couple of months she came up with partial rent, promising to get caught up, which she never did and I finally had to evict her.

## Wendy's Wisdom

*See why I can write this book? I have made all the mistakes, so you don't have to!*

*I've done many things right over the years, and that is what you should follow in this book. If you follow this book, you will have minimal problems, and hopefully none.*

Whether you are feeling the pain of your mortgage payment or the tenant-buyer has a story for why they need to move in quickly, you still have to screen your tenant-buyers. If you don't screen them fully, the odds are very heavily favored for you having to do an eviction.

**Manage Your Tenants, Don't Let Them Manage You**

Once you have tenant-buyers in your home you become a landlord. If you are using a property manager – good for you. If you want a property manager, but you don't have one – check out my rent-to-own site for a property manager near you or email me at refer@wendypatton.com. They will be found in the real estate agents section. A property manager can make your life much easier.

If you are managing the tenants yourself, you need to act like a landlord. Be fair, but firm. The rules are spelled out in the rental agreement, and both you and the tenants need to abide by those rules.

As soon as you start letting things slide, the tenants will start walking all over you. Make that little bit of effort to ensure they stay in line, and you'll find you have far fewer headaches when dealing with tenants.

## Wendy's Wisdom

*Don't be afraid of having tenants. They won't walk all over you if you put in a little effort to enforce the terms of the rental agreement. Trust me, it really is a little effort, but you need to do it.*

### Use the Right Contracts

Using the right contracts, like the ones I offer on my website, will make life so much easier for you. You will get far more legal protection than standard contracts offer, which becomes very important if you have any problems. Because they are pro-seller contracts they will also save you money, sometimes many thousands of dollars.

*Getting the right contracts to use is a small investment that pays off with big returns.*

**Have an Attorney Review Your Paperwork**

It's always a good idea to make use of an attorney when it comes to dealing with legally binding paperwork. I may make some jokes about attorneys in this book, but that doesn't mean I don't value their legal expertise. Remember the adage "An ounce of prevention is worth a pound of cure"? In this case, an ounce of attorney time now in reviewing your contracts can be worth many pounds of dollars saved in legal fees down the road.

If you don't want to spend thousands of dollars for an attorney, definitely sign up for Pre-Paid Legal, it is referenced in the appendix of this book. The savings are tremendous.

**Don't Get Discouraged by "No-Offer" Showings**

I see this happen with all types of home sellers, rent-to-own or others. After multiple showings without an offer, they start to let things slide. They don't make as much effort to keep their home clean, and they are not so quick to return phone calls. After a while they stop making efforts almost altogether.

This will not get your home sold. You have to stay consistent with your efforts. Sometimes selling a home takes time. Selling it on a rent-to-own basis can certainly help speed up the process, but it still may take time to find the right tenant-buyer.

Remember, each showing or phone call you get could be the right person. You need to give the last showing as much effort as the first showing.

**Keep Tabs on Your Tenant-Buyer's Credit Progress**

Check in with your tenant-buyer periodically to make sure they are on track toward rebuilding their credit. Don't get invasive, but also don't be totally negligent. If you use my contracts you also have the right to pull their credit report during the rental period, so you can check to see how their credit score is improving. Pulling credit too often actually damages the score, so you don't want to overdo it.

## Use the Help of Professionals

Real estate agents, mortgage brokers, tax advisors, property managers, and attorneys are all professionals that can help you with the sale of your rent-to-own home. Their expertise will make your life significantly easier. They can guide you away from making a lot of mistakes, some of which can have legal consequences.

Don't try to do this all by yourself. It just makes it a whole lot more work for you and in the end, it will probably end up costing you more with the mistakes you make than if you had sought the help of professionals in the first place.

*Get help in the beginning, not after it's too late*

### Don't Stagger Your Marketing

When you are advertising your home, you want to do all of the free and nearly free marketing at the same time. Don't do one for a while and then say, "Well, that didn't work" and move onto another, and so on. You will have much greater success by getting all of your marketing out there. You'll have more showings and find your tenant-buyer sooner.

### Make Sure Your Pricing is Realistic

I usually can tell why a home hasn't gotten much interest just from looking at the ad. Unfortunately most sellers want to get their mortgage payment or more in rent, but many times the rental rates for the area are much lower. Be competitive with what you are asking for rent and for your option fee. If you ask too much, you will be asking for a long time.

**Your Goal** →

Remember your Goal:
Get your home SOLD!

### Get Started by Taking Small Steps

I saved this one for last, because it's now time for you to go out and take action. The key to successfully selling your rent-to-own home is to **get started**. The best way for you to get started is by taking it one step at a time.

The quickest way to fail is to feel overwhelmed. Focus on individual steps, and you will find the task very simple and easy to handle. Just remember: one step at a time and you can sell your home. If it seems too overwhelming, definitely have a real estate agent help you. As Plato said, "The beginning is the most important part of the work." I wish you the best with your rent-to-own experience!

# PART 7

## FOR THE REAL ESTATE
## AGENT ONLY

# Chapter 22

## When and How to Recommend
## Renting-to-Own to Your Seller

As real estate agents, we know that it can be more difficult, often much more difficult, to sell homes in a down real estate market. Obviously rent-to-own isn't the first choice for you or your seller, but the first choice (selling homes outright) isn't working very well right now given the real estate market and mortgage industry. Nevertheless, the sellers we represent still need to get their homes sold. This is where good agents provide alternatives, and the other agents lose their listings.

Everything in this book is for working with home sellers. For home buyers you'll want to reference my book, _Rent-to-Buy_ (for buyers). Both are excellent resources and should be a part of any real estate agent's reference materials.

### Wendy's Wisdom

_The purpose of this technique is to provide an alternative to your sellers when their home hasn't sold fast enough using conventional methods._

Rent-to-Sell Checklist for Realtors®

- ☐ Talk to the seller about rent-to-own:
    - o explain rent-to-own
    - o go over risks and rewards
- ☐ Help them determine if rent-to-own is right for them
- ☐ Update the Listing Agreement
- ☐ Have them sign the Seller's Acknowledgement

☐ Keep in touch with the mortgage lender and credit repair agency to make sure the tenant-buyer are on track

☐ See the seller's checklist in Chapter 16. Make sure those items are completed.

### When Should You Talk with Your Seller About Rent-to-Own?

The best time to mention other creative strategies to your seller for selling their home is during your listing presentation. This lets the seller know that you have alternatives available if their home has trouble selling in the conventional way. Being able to discuss these alternatives will set you apart from other listing agents and may help you get the listing. Today it isn't enough to just "get a listing." We must be able to sell a listing. Selling listings today requires agents to understand and know more creative strategies.

> I always say to real estate agents:
> "Will you be here in 5 years or gone in 5 months?"
>
> Only creative agents will prosper during down markets.

You will want to remind the seller of the alternatives down the road if their home hasn't sold. You should do this before they get too frustrated with the lack of results. Any listings that you already have that are not selling are good candidates to consider an alternative. A rent-to-own or lease-to-own is one of the alternatives you should be discussing with your seller. If you don't, the seller is going to get frustrated and may switch agents, or may insist on renting their home. You want to present them with alternatives to consider before they reach this point.

If the seller says to you, "If you don't sell my home soon I'm going to have to rent it," you know this seller is a good candidate for rent-to-own. You'll make more in commission than if you just found a renter for them.

## How Should You Discuss Rent-to-Own with Your Seller?

When you have this conversation with your seller you should be direct, particularly if you didn't mention it in the listing presentation. You can say something like, "Here's the situation. We know the market isn't great right now. It's a lot slower than it used to be which is making it a lot harder to sell your home. It's time to consider some alternatives. How much longer do you want your home to sit on the market? Do you want to reduce the price or consider alternative methods of selling? You may want to think about selling your home on a rent-to-own basis. You can usually get a better price and may also find a buyer a lot sooner." If they express interest, discuss potential risks they should take into consideration, which we'll cover in the next chapter.

You can discuss other alternatives with the seller as well, not just rent-to-own. Some other options include:

- Contract for deed (a.k.a. Land Contract)

- Holding a second mortgage

- Offering to pay closing costs or buy down mortgage points

Do some research on these methods if you are not familiar with them.

## Which Sellers Can Consider Rent-to-Own?

When you look at the sellers of your current listings or the sellers of listings you are trying to get, take into account their situation before mentioning rent-to-own. It does not work for everyone. However, there are many types of sellers that can consider rent-to-own.

- *When their home has been on the market for 90 days or longer.* Slow selling homes can be good candidates for rent-to-own because sellers become more open minded to other ideas as they see their home languishing on the market.

263

- *Seller has already moved into their new home.* Whether the seller bought or built a new home and the old one hasn't sold yet, they have two homes and two house payments. No seller wants to pay for a home to sit empty for very long.

- *Relocated to a new area.* If a seller has relocated and their old home hasn't sold yet.

- *New marriage.* If the newlyweds were both homeowners and they move into one house and are selling the other.

- *Owe as much on their home as it's worth.* This lack of equity makes it difficult for a seller to sell their home outright because they'll have to bring money to closing. However, a rent-to-own home may bring a price premium that can cover some or all of this difference. Plus, the additional time of the rental period may allow the seller to pay down more principal on their mortgage. Remember: can it pay your commission too?

- *Own free and clear.* Free and clear sellers aren't burdened with the extra mortgage payment, but they also aren't in the position where their home must be sold immediately. Even if they need money from their home, they can always take out an equity loan during the rental period, or before they rent-to-own their home.

- *Landlord selling a rental property.* Landlords can make great rent-to-own sellers since they are already used to the idea of tenants. Also, because the home isn't their primary residence, they aren't likely to need the money from the sale right away.
- *Inherited the property.* Recently inherited property is usually sitting empty and the owners may not need the money right away. This works well with one or two heirs, but when you have many heirs, it tends to get more difficult to get them all to agree to anything.

- *Vacation home or 2nd home.* Because this isn't the seller's principal residence, the home may be sitting empty, and they may be making two mortgage payments. Getting it rented will give the seller some cash each month they don't have now.

## Wendy's Wisdom

*This is NOT a good solution for a seller that is excessively upside down on the value of their home and what they owe. Think about the end of the deal. Will they be able to bring the extra money to the table that will be owed in the mortgage and for your commission? If they are upside down, they should consider a short sale on their home, not option it to someone.*

You'll notice that many good rent-to-own candidates have two things in common:

1. They have a home sitting empty (and)

2. They don't need the money from the sale right away

Bear in mind that there is a difference between *needing* the money right away and *wanting* the money right away.

Homeowners that are selling their principal residence and still living in it are potential candidates as well. They just need to make sure that they will still be able to get a mortgage on their new home while renting their old home. Lending requirements are tougher on this type situation than in past years. Have them get pre-approved with a lender for this situation prior to going too far.

**Which Sellers are Able to do Rent-to-Own?**

We have established criteria for sellers that can consider rent-to-own but not all of them are actually able. Here are some examples where sellers who could, or would, consider rent-to-own, but are probably not good candidates to do so. This is where protecting yourself, the buyer and the brokerage come into play. This book teaches how to work with sellers, and I assume you are a seller's agent while reading this book. You still want to make sure it is a viable deal for all involved, however, and that includes the buyers.

1. *Short sale situation.* Sellers that are on the brink of foreclosure and owe more than the house is worth are not likely to be able to do rent-to-own. They might want to do this, or think they can. Think about what could happen down the road when the tenant-buyer decides to buy, and the seller doesn't have the money for the shortage to bring to the closing. What then? It would be a mess for sure and we don't like messes! Not to mention you may not get paid!

2. *Behind on payments.* Sellers that are behind on payments might be okay, if they can get caught up and are not too upside-down on their home. Sometimes with the help of the option fee, or some other means, the seller can get caught up. In this situation, you would want a third party (setting up escrow) to make the mortgage payments directly instead of trusting the seller to do so. That is crucial to making things work. The buyer could, technically, also make the payments, but you need to make sure you are protecting your seller, as well as the buyer, for this scenario.

3. *Live in Texas.* This is a reminder in case you didn't catch it in the main part of the book. Texas State law makes it difficult to do rent-to-own home sales.

4. *Will the rent cover their mortgage?* If the seller's mortgage payments are higher than the monthly rent, they would have to cover the difference each month themselves. Are they in a situation to do this? It is a must to make this scenario work. They can do a rent-to-own if they can cover this difference. For example: if the rent is $1,200 per month and the seller's mortgage payment is $1,397 per month, the seller would need to pay $197 each month for the shortage. This is another case where it may be a good idea to set up an escrow

account to ensure the mortgage is actually getting paid. The buyer would pay in $1,200 each month and the seller would pay in $197 each month plus any escrow fee charges.

## Wendy's Wisdom

*You are not doing your seller any favor by trying to ask for a rental rate high enough to cover their mortgage payment if it is above market rent.*

Market rent is what it is and you can't change that for them. In other words, if you try to market a home above what it is worth, it won't sell. This is the same situation. It must be marketed where it will rent. Remind the seller that if their entire payment, plus their utilities, is a lot more than the shortage, they will need to make up each month.

Sometimes it is necessary to put that into perspective to help your seller see the other side. I can't tell you how many real estate agents I talk to about doing a rent-to-own just assume the mortgage payment of the seller should be the asking price for rent. This would be a mistake for your seller, so think through this before you get them thinking in the wrong direction, and then they become disappointed about not selling their home at all.

So what can you do if your seller can't afford to cover that difference each month? Are your sellers out of luck?

Not necessarily. Here's an idea to get buyer's to pay more in monthly rent, which will work if your seller has equity in their home. When you are advertising the home, advertise for market rent. Once you find a buyer that wants the home and have met with them, review their application to see if they can pay more per month based on their income. If they can, ask them, "Would you like to earn 50% on your money?"

They would probably say, "Yes!" or "What do you mean?"

267

I would respond by saying, "If you pay $200 more in rent each month, meaning $1,400 instead of $1,200, the sellers will give you that $200 each month as an option credit on this home, plus an additional $100 option credit. This would give you a 50% return on your money and help you buy this home much more quickly by building up option credits. Would this work for you?"

This gives your seller an extra $200 per month to cover the mortgage payment, but they will credit it back to the tenant-buyer at closing. If the tenant-buyer doesn't purchase the home, the seller keeps the extra money.

Obviously you need to discuss this with your seller in advance and determine if it would work for them. You might also want to get legal advice for your area on giving option credits. This could be a problem if your area is very pro-tenant and judges consider this as *equitable interest*. *Equitable interest* is not a problem unless the tenant-buyer doesn't pay and your seller has to remove them from the home. If this happens then they might have to foreclose versus evict if the judge determines they have *equitable interest*. This is fairly rare, but something you must not overlook.

You, as an agent, need to be cautious of creating liability for you, the seller, and your brokerage. Not just with option credits and *equitable interest*, but in everything pertaining to the rent-to-own transaction. You want to protect your sellers as much as possible, but there are some risks when doing this type of real estate transaction. Actually, there is risk in any type of real estate transaction. We just sometimes forget that point when we are trying something new. You need to understand the risks. In the next chapter we will discuss the risks to discuss with your seller when doing a rent-to-own.

*If you never take a risk you will never reap the reward.*

# Chapter 23

# Having the Rewards and Risks Discussion with Your Seller

When you discuss rent-to-own with your sellers, you need to cover the potential risks as well as the rewards. It is important to make sure the seller understands both so they can evaluate them as part of their decision to sell their home on a rent-to-own basis. Which one do you want first, the good news or the bad news?

Ok, we will go with the bad news (the risks) before we cover the benefits. There are several risks to you and your sellers in a rent-to-own transaction.

*Risks*

Included below is a checklist that covers the potential risks. Don't just hand your seller the checklist to initial and sign. You should review each item with them. Don't over-hype rent-to-own to your sellers; keep it realistic. Portray the risks in a fair light. They can easily be pretty gloomy if you don't keep them realistic.

Sometimes these risks can scare your sellers to the point of no return, but you still must cover them. This is why you want to keep them realistic. Many of the risks with the tenants can be greatly mitigated by proper screening and using property management. In other words, the chances of these risks happening are fairly slim with proper screening, but they can still happen.

# Acknowledgments for Sellers for a Rent-to-Own Transaction

*Dated* _____

_____ I/We understand that the tenant-buyer may stop paying rent and I might need to evict them.

_____ I/We understand that I may receive very little to no money up front depending on the option fee and my commission agreement with my real estate broker.

_____ I/We understand that the tenant-buyer might move out and do damage to my home.

_____ I/We understand that the tenant-buyer might not purchase my home.

_____ I/We understand that my property taxes may change when I have a renter in my home.

_____ I/We understand that my homeowner's insurance may change (or that I may need to make changes to my policy).

_____ I/We have read everything above and understand and accept these risks.

_____ I/We will hold the broker (XYZ) harmless for anything from the above list that goes wrong with my rent-to-own transaction.

_____        _____
Signature                        Signature

## Wendy's Wisdom

*This is very important. Have your broker and/or the attorney for your office review and approve this checklist before you use it with any of your clients or customers. Most real estate agents must review contract additions and changes with an attorney.*

*Real estate agents can benefit tremendously from Pre-Paid Legal services, as well as their clients. Check it out at www.Prepaidlegal.com/hub/wendypatton - to save you legal fees and time.*

You can go to www.WendyPatton.com/checklist to download the above list.

### Let's Review Some of These Risks

_____ *I/We understand that the tenant-buyer may stop paying rent and I might need to evict them.*

Evictions are always a possibility when you have tenants, however, they are fairly rare (if they were that common no one would be willing to rent in the first place). Additionally, the chance of needing to do an eviction can be greatly reduced by conducting proper tenant screening when the tenant-buyer submits his application, as well as properly managing the tenant when they are living in the home. Sellers will be much better off using a property manager. This reduces the chances of needing to evict and places the responsibility of handling any eviction with the property manager. If you are not a property manager, help your sellers find a good one with a good reputation. Unfortunately, good property managers are not so easy find, so check around.

If the seller does elect to self–manage, and find he needs to evict his tenant, he should make use of an eviction attorney. The best way to find one is through your local real estate investor's association. Not only are these attorneys usually very experienced, but they typically handle evictions in bulk so the rate is less expensive.

_____ ***I/We understand that I may receive very little to no money up front depending on the option fee and my commission agreement with my real estate broker.***

Typically you will negotiate a partial commission payment paid when the tenant-buyers take possession of the property, which is typically paid out of the option fee. This usually means that there isn't too much left over for the seller, if any. However, in most situations for rent-to-own sellers their home was sitting vacant. This means they aren't really losing anything since they weren't getting anything in the first place.

_____ ***I/We understand that the tenant-buyer might move out and do damage to my home.***

Collecting a small security deposit from the tenant-buyers can be helpful for recovering any damages. Plus, in most states, you can pursue legal action against buyers to recover damages. You, as the real estate agent, should check to see what the laws are in your area to know what options for recourse your seller has (a local property manager will know for sure). This way, you have the answers for your seller in advance. Also, find out if the property manager you recommend will pursue this judgment and collection for your seller. Some will do this for their clients, but many will not.

_____ ***I/We understand that the tenant-buyer might not purchase my home.***

If this happens, the seller may need to put his home up for sale again, either conventionally or as a rent-to-own. This may actually be advantageous, however, if the market has turned around and values start climbing again. Also, point out that at least there was someone paying them a monthly payment during the rent-to-own period, which is much better than them paying for the home to sit empty.

_____ *I/We understand that my property taxes may change when I have a renter in my home.*

Some states have different property tax rates for owner-occupied versus tenant-occupied properties. As the real estate agent, you should know whether or not this will happen to your seller. You should also know exactly how it could affect them.

_____ *I/We understand that my homeowner's insurance may change (or that I may need to make changes to my policy).*

Insurance should be changed by the seller to reflect that a tenant now occupies the property and it is not owner occupied. It will depend on the location of their home, but insurance can go up, go down, or stay close to the same.

_____ *I/We have read everything above and understand and accept these risks.*

_____ *I/We will hold the broker (XYZ) harmless for anything from the above list that goes wrong with my rent-to-own transaction.*

Put your broker's name in this versus XYZ, it will be easier for the seller to understand ☺. This is just one of our great CYA clauses we need as real estate agents and brokers.

## Benefits

It is important to cover the benefits to the seller as well. You might want to start out with these, or mention the risks, and then review the benefits. It will depend on your style and your seller. Help them to understand how rent-to-own can get their home sold when it might not otherwise sell, or keep their home from sitting on the market for a very long time. I cover a lot of benefits throughout this book, but I'm going to focus on the three primary ones here.

### An Almost **Must** *in Our Market*

One of the first benefits is that this option often is almost a necessity. Rent-to-own has really almost become a *must* in our real estate market. Buyers are having tremendous difficulties obtaining financing, and large numbers of sellers are competing for the few qualified buyers. Rent-to-own expands far beyond the small pool of buyers that can obtain mortgages right now. If sellers want to sell their home quickly, they really need to consider rent-to-own.

### Higher Sales Price

Another benefit is that a seller can receive a higher sales price. Rent-to-owns often command a price premium over conventional sales. Plus, tenant-buyers typically have less negotiating capability because of the huge level of flexibility they are being offered with rent-to-own. To put it bluntly: Buyers have less room to negotiate when they need the seller to do a rent-to-own.

That's a lot more desirable than having buyers take advantage of sellers with ridiculously low offers, given the current market.

### Sell Quicker

Lastly, your sellers may be able to sell much quicker when they expand their pool of buyers. By expanding their reach to a greater number of potential buyers, they are much more likely to find the right buyer sooner. Additionally, once they have found a tenant-buyer the screening and approval process is much shorter than a conventional buyer applying for a mortgage, so they can get the tenant moved in much faster.

So your seller has told you they are open to this idea, or you already know they might need this type of a solution. Are you worried about how and when you will be paid? I am sure you are. After all, as much as we like to help our sellers out we still need to get paid for our work. We will discuss how you get paid in the next chapter.

# Chapter 24

## How to Get Paid Your Entire Commission and More

Don't tell me you flipped to this chapter before Chapter 1? I bet some of you did.

You might want to find out more about what this all means and how it is done before you worry about how to get paid. Getting paid is crucial for everyone. I can help you figure out how to make 100% of your earned commission and potentially more where you might otherwise have lost a listing or just gotten paid for renting a home.

The reality is that conventional sales are difficult right now. It isn't enough to just get listings and put them on the market, because most of them aren't selling. The number of licensed agents will continue to drop as the market stays down. The main reason? It is not because there are not enough real estate transactions, but because too many agents are not willing to learn what must be done in today's market. They are not willing to find out how to do the transactions that are needed in today's marketplace. They do not *shift* with the market (a great book by Gary Keller, Jay Papasan and Dave Jenks – SHIFT).

Some agents are whining and making excuses versus getting out there and figuring out how to make things work. Obviously, you are not one of them if you are reading this book. Make sure you add SHIFT to your reference list.

We, as agents, have gotten lazy. I will try not to get on a soapbox, but since I am writing this book it gives me a little leeway. Most real estate agents rarely come to their office meetings, and rarely go to training to learn new concepts. What I talk about in this book, I teach to real estate offices across the country. They invite the agents for weeks and weeks to come to my training session. Ninety short minutes and only 20% of their office will show up. Why? Because 20% of the agents do 80% of the business. I have recently talked to some owners of offices and they say now 10% of their agents do about 90% of the business.

If you want to keep succeeding in this business you **must adapt**. Not only are rent-to-owns going to be very popular, but seller financing is making a big come back. That is a topic for another book. Agents that offer rent-to-own sales will have much more success selling homes than agents that try to hold out for only conventional buyers.

## Wendy's Wisdom

*You'll retain more listings, get more listings, get more buyers and ultimately get paid more if you offer your sellers creative solutions.*

Let's look specifically at one of your listings that has been sitting on the market for a while. Odds are the seller is starting to get frustrated with the lack of results. At this point, if you only stick to conventional sales one of three things will happen:

1. *You get the seller to agree to a price reduction.* This may or may not be enough to get the home sold, if they can even afford to do it. If they do agree, they aren't going to be too happy about it. However, if they can reduce the price to get it sold, then it is probably the best thing for them and you.

2. *The seller switches agents* thinking that another agent may be able to get their home sold. Most sellers think it is the agent doing a good or not-so-good job that sells or doesn't sell their home. They know the market is bad, but many sellers think (well, they believe) that their home is the BEST on the market. Therefore, many of them blame the lack of selling their home on you, their real estate agent.

3. *The seller decides to rent their home.* You didn't hear the seller say the dreaded 4 letter word? "Real estate agent, if you don't sell my home soon, I am going to have to RENT it." If you ignored that or didn't know how to respond, you probably ended up letting the seller just rent their home, and you may or may not have even been paid to help with that transaction. What does a rental pay? Not much! Do you want an entire commission or a portion of a month's rent?

### How to Get Paid Your Entire Commission

None of the above options are really all that attractive. Consider this instead:

With a rent-to-own you still get your full commission (and maybe more, which I'll get into shortly) plus the seller gets a better price for their home instead of having to do a price drop. This means more for your seller and more for you.

There is a string attached, which is that you'll only get part of your commission up front (but still more than if you just rented the property) and the remainder when the tenant-buyer closes on the

279

home. The same goes for the seller; they may get a small amount of money at the beginning, and the rest when the home is sold.

## Change Your Listing Agreement

When a seller decides they want to list their home as a rent-to-own you will need to change the listing agreement with the seller. Any changes you make should be verified by your broker and, if necessary, your office's legal counsel.

Here are some of the changes you'll need to make. Usually they can be typed on a one page addendum, or handwritten in, and signed by the broker and the seller:

- *Seller agrees to pay listing broker X% commission of the purchase price if listing broker secures a rent-to-own tenant-buyer by dd/mm/yy.*

- *Seller agrees to pay commission to listing office even if tenant-buyer's rent-to-own agreement is extended one or more times.* (In other words no matter when your tenant-buyer closes, you still get paid – even if it is 10 years from now.)

- *Seller agrees to pay listing broker 2% of the contract purchase price from proceeds of the option fee received by the tenant-buyer at the time the tenant-buyer moves in.* (Of course this is negotiable with your seller, but it's what I recommend, because most buyers only have 1-2% down.) Any amount above the 2% received by the tenant-buyer would be retained by the seller. This 2% would apply towards the entire commission due on this home, if and when, the tenant-buyer closes on the home.

## How to Get MORE than Your Normal Commission

You may also choose to ask the seller for additional commission if a rent-to-own buyer is secured due to all of the extra work necessary. For example, if you normally would receive 6% commission you might ask for 7% if you can find a rent-to-own buyer. This is a premium level of service not offered by many other agents. Want to justify it real quick? Have them read this book and see what is involved. Then ask, "Would you like to do this, or would you like me to take care of this for you? I am sure you don't have time for all for this. That is why you hired me in the first place, right?"

Other reasons they should pay more: You may need to do additional advertising for the rent-to-own. You will also need to keep an eye on things during the option period, ensuring the tenant-buyer is getting credit repair done, is working with a lender, and will be able to purchase the home. Additional justification is that by selling as a rent-to-own your sellers will be able to sell for a higher purchase price than conventional sale, thereby getting them more money. I believe the value you contribute is worth more than a traditional sale. This is up to you, your broker and your seller.

## Wendy's Wisdom

*Offering sellers an option such as rent-to-own truly is a premium level of service.*

*You'll be able to help the sellers get their home sold (and at a better price) when other agents didn't.*

One thing you will need to consider is if a buyer's agent brings you a tenant-buyer. How will you split that 2% upfront commission payment (as in my example)? This is up to you as the listing agent/broker. You can offer whatever you want to the selling office in your MLS listing, or however you offer compensation to the selling office. You might offer 1% or you might offer as little as

281

½ months rent. These are just examples, but something for you to consider. In my book, _Rent-to-Buy_ (for buyers), I will share with real estate agents how to get ½ of that upfront commission and how to get the listing agreement changed to accommodate them (of course you might have to go back to your seller for anything you and the other agent agree to that is not already part of the listing agreement).

Now, that you understand how you'll get paid, go back to Chapter 1 and read the entire book so you can help your sellers do this type of transaction☺. Be different and take on this market instead of letting this market take you!

# Appendix A

## Helpful Resources

### Available at www.WendyPatton.com

- *Rent-to-Sell* Course - Contracts for sellers doing a rent-to-own, with audio CDs containing step-by-step instructions

- *Rent-to-Buy* Course - Contracts for buyers doing a rent-to-own, with audio CDs containing step-by-step instructions

- Realtor® and Mortgage Broker Contacts for your area

- Credit Repair Contacts for your Tenant-Buyers

- Credit Report and Criminal background check sites

- **FREE** Downloads of the Checklists from this book

  www.WendyPatton.com/Checklists

- **FREE** articles on rent-to-own

### Other Sites:

- http://www.cpsc.gov/cpscpub/pubs/426.pdf
Protect your family from lead in your home pamphlet. Must be given to buyers and renters as part of Lead Based Paint Disclosure.

- www.craigslist.org

A resource for listing your rent-to-own home. Also a good resource for finding free or inexpensive home improvement materials and moving boxes.

- www.craigslist.org/about/FHA#categories

A state-by-state description of what classes are protected by law from housing discrimination.

- www.familywatchdog.us/default.asp

Free search for convicted sex offenders by name or location.

- www.freecycle.org

A good resource for finding free home improvement materials and moving boxes.

- Pre-Paid                                                      Legal
  www.prepaidlegal.com/hub/wendypatton

For affordable legal assistance with no contract required.

- www.RenttoOwnCreditRepair.com

A great source for credit repair. Get your tenant-buyer signed up as soon as they sign a contract with you.

Please feel free to email my office with **<u>success stories</u>** of selling your home using my rent-to-own system. Email my office at: <u>success@wendypatton.com</u>.

Share with us in this format:

Subject Line: Success Story for a Rent-to-Own Seller

1.  Your name(s)

2.  What city you live in

3.  What you did to sell your home

4.  How long did it take before you tried this?

5.  What you liked about the rent-to-own over selling your home outright (for instance did you get more money)?

6.  Can I use your name(s) and success story on my website to share with others who need rent-to-own as a solution to sell their home?

# Continue Your Education

Now that you know how to do rent-to-own as a seller, would you like to learn how to do this as a buyer?

If so, you can purchase *Rent-to-Buy* (for buyers) on my website at www.WendyPatton.com.

You can also do rent-to-owns as a **little to no money down real estate investing technique**. If you are interested in real estate investing, you can receive a FREE CD from me one of three ways:

- You can sign up for the FREE CD at www.WendyPatton.com or

- You can email your contact information to: support@wendypatton.com

- You can also fax the following form to

248-605-4044.

Wendy, please rush me my free CD!

Name: _____

Email: _____

Are you a Realtor®?   Yes      or        No

What Company:_____

Address: _____

City: _____

State: _____Zip: _____

Cell phone: _____

Daytime phone:_____


What are your goals for learning to invest in real estate?

_____

_____

_____

_____

_____

_____

# Wendy Patton

Wendy Patton is widely recognized as one of the most inspiring speakers on "Little or No Money Down" real estate investing. Her real estate savvy, great depth of experience and viable knowledge has helped her in orchestrating the most complete and easy to follow Lease Option & Subject To program in the country.

After graduating from the University of Colorado, Wendy went to work for EDS. Soon after, she had an enlightening experience in real estate (lease/option) and walked away from her corporate job to focus her efforts on real estate investing full-time.

Wendy is a licensed real estate broker in 3 states and licensed builder in Michigan. With over 23 successful years in general real estate and hundreds of transactions using lease option, or renting-to-own, she is the country's leading expert on lease options and working with Realtors to acquire lease option deals. Wendy loves to teach others and assist them to achieve the same level of success that she has personally experienced.

Wendy Patton is a published author and well known public speaker. Her first book, Investing in Real Estate with Lease Options and Subject To Deals – Powerful Strategies for Getting More When You Sell and Paying Less When You Buy, has received rave reviews on Amazon.com and other real estate investor websites. Her second book came out in August 2007 and was immediately a #1 Best Seller on Amazon.com. How to Make Hard Cash in a Soft Real Estate Market. She also recently appeared on HGTV's, *My House IS Worth What?*

Wendy has been an educator and speaker on real estate investing since 1995. She is an avid golfer and currently lives in the Detroit suburb of Clarkston, Michigan with her husband, Michael Gott, and their 5 children.

**For more information on Wendy Patton, please visit**
www.wendypatton.com.

# NOTES

[i] Recognizing that families have a right to know about lead-based paint and potential lead hazards in their homes, Congress directed EPA and HUD to work together to develop disclosure requirements for sales and leases of older housing. These requirements became effective in 1996. EPA has established hazard standards for paints, dust, and soil in most pre-1978 housing and child-occupied facilities. These requirements became effective in 2001. Brochure available at http://www.epa.gov/lead/pubs/fs-discl.pdf Sample disclosure form available at http://www.epa.gov/lead/pubs/lesr_eng.pdf.

[ii] The International Association of Home Staging Professionals® is the professional association serving the Home Staging industry. Since 1999, IAHSP has set high standards based on educational requirements, standards of excellence, and a code of ethics for members as they service the public in the communities where they live and work. IAHSP is open to all Home Stagers that meet the educational standards set for membership.